A MUSLIM'S
Guide to American
POLITICS &
GOVERNMENT

2nd Edition

RAEED N. TAYEH

Muslim American Society (MAS)

Falls Church, VA

A Muslim's Guide to American Politics and Government

Second Edition, 2004

Raeed N. Tayeh
Email: Raeed@masnet.org

© Copyright 2002-2004
Muslim American Society
P.O. Box 1896
Falls Church, VA 22041
Tel: (703) 998-6525
Fax: (703) 998-6526
Email: mas@masnet.org
URL: www.masnet.org

ISBN 0-9760772-05
Library of Congress Control Number: 2004111497

Printed in the United States of America by
International Graphics,
10710 Tucker Street
Beltsville, MD 20705
Tel. (301) 595-5999
www.igprinting.com

TABLE OF CONTENTS

ILLUSTRATIONS

FOREWORD

In the name of Allah, most Gracious, most Merciful. All praise is due to Almighty Allah, the master of the day of judgement and the controller of the earths and the heavens and the prayers and blessings be upon the last of Allah's messenger, prophet Muhammed.

The Muslim American Society (MAS) envisions itself as a most invigorating and dynamic organization that espouses the comprehensive understanding of Islam as its mission and way of life and whose members are examplery citizens of this nation. Examplery citizens, who shoulder to shoulder with their fellow Americans, are working to make this great nation a more just and principled nation, a nation that is not only true to its founding fathers' ideals, but also whose practices set the standards of justice and prosperity for the American people and for the rest of the world.

In attaining that vision, MAS works through a process of comprehensive reform through the dual paradigm of outreach and development. Our development strategy operates both at the level of the individual and the level of the community. At the individual level, we aim to develop the principled, disciplined and self-motivated individual whose life's compass is attaining the pleasure of Allah SWT. At the community level, we aim to empower the community so that it can fulfill its obligation of serving as witnesses upon mankind as carriers of the guidance of Allah SWT.

One of the most important components of the development of the community through empowerment is indeed political empowerment. We in MAS believe that our obligation to empower our community through political involvement stems from understanding our obligations as Muslims. Understanding the political system of our country is the first step towards the political empowerment of our community that is so vital to our ultimate goal of raising and developing these examplery citizens who will contribute to the greatness of our country and whose convictions and dedication will illuminate the brilliance and beauty of the great message of Islam.

By understanding American politics and government at its basics, we will be empowered to construct the most effective political strategy and develop the most relevant political discourse to make our community not only visible and active but also able and productive. In fulfillment of our Islamic duty to enjoin the good and forbid the evil, we must be empowered politically and we must be committed Islamically. By understanding the political system that runs this country, we can achieve the progress we need to bring about an appreciation and inclusion of our ideals and our identity as people who profess to be a modern and recent rendition of monotheism and who believe that the guidance of Allah SWT is for all who are part of the brotherhood of humanity.

Dr. Esam Omeish

President, Muslim American Society (MAS)

PREFACE

The Muslim community in the United States of America has gone through many phases over the years, and it continues to develop as the fastest growing and most diverse religious community in the nation. With these developments have come hardships and opportunities. Muslim-Americans have the opportunity in this country, unlike any other in the Muslim world, to engage the political system that affects their lives, to influence it, and to benefit from it.

Government is a system that people in society form in order to provide things that individuals may not be able to provide on their own, like defense from harm and fraud, clean drinking water, education, and so on. The policies that governments adopt change over time, but the functions of government remain the same.

Politics is the series of relationships between people that makes the government function, and it determines who gets what, when, and how: who gets the jobs, education, housing, healthcare, and justice. Politics determines who the government spends its money, your tax dollars, with, and it determines which programs to fund and where to implement those programs.

Engaging the American political system is important to Muslims because of issues that concern them at home and abroad. American foreign policy is probably the greatest concern for most immigrants and their American-born children, while domestic issues like education, civil rights, and the economy might be of greater concern to indigenous Muslim whose ancestors have been in America for generations.

Whatever the issue may be, one must fully understand the political system that runs this country. Therefore Muslim-Americans, particularly those who are very passionate about their issues and wish to become community activists, must learn about the origin, structure, and role of the American government, the politics that shape it, and the institutions that affect it the most.

This book is designed as an introduction to all of these topics. It will, insha'Allah, give you a basic understanding of how the government functions and how it is influenced. There is much to explain and many questions to answer, but this book will stay on course with its defined goals of presenting clear and concise knowledge about the federal, state, and local governments, political parties, the voting process, and the role of interest groups in politics. This second edition of the book features new sections packed with useful resources, activist tools, and solid advice. After obtaining this knowledge you will be better prepared to take an active role in the Muslim community, as well as in your community in general.

This book should become the basis for the further study of politics, and it should serve as a guide that you can refer to when a general question arises about American politics or government. You should not assume that everything you need to know about American politics is in this book.

Political Vision for Muslim-Americans

Many Muslims think that their community is politically weak, and that they cannot change governmental policy because of a number of reasons: The Zionists control everything; the West does not accept Islam and Muslims; politics is a waste of time and resources; Muslims will never work together for the common good; etc. All of these may seem like valid points to someone who does not know about the political system and how it works, but for the informed Muslim, these reasons are just simplistic answers to complicated problems. American Jews are very powerful--this is true--but they do not maintain their power through secret conspiracies designed to control everything in this country. This does not mean that many elements of the Jewish community do not plot against Muslims and their interests; they do. But overall, they are as powerful as they are because they understand how the system works, and they know how to use it to their advantage. It has taken them over 100 years to get this powerful, however, while the Muslim-American community has been on the map for only 30 or 40 years. If you compare the development of both communities, you will see that the Muslim community has reached the point where it is now much faster than the Jews did. If this trend continues, Muslims in America will be a major political force within several years if they continue on the course that they are on now. So one should think positively about the political future of Muslims, not negatively.

The Muslim students of today will be the politicians and journalists of tomorrow; today's lawyers will become tomorrow's judges; and those who have power now will be weak in the future. All you have to do is be patient, determined, and active, for as the Qur'an says: "Oh you who believe, seek guidance through patience and prayer, for Allah is with those who are patient." *(Surah 2, verse 153).*

9

"Tip" O'Neill, the late Speaker of the House of Representatives, once said, "All politics is local." This little phrase is so powerful because it is so true. Whatever happens in Washington depends on how the constituents of congressmen and senators feel back home in their districts and states. This lesson will be very clear by the end of this book.

Raeed N. Tayeh

CHAPTER 1

A NATION IS BORN

In 1492 AD, Christopher Columbus sailed from Spain with three ships in search of a shortcut to India that would make the importation of spices and other items much cheaper. Instead of traveling the long way over land from Asia to Europe, there would be a direct water route that shippers could use without paying a lot of commission for different stages of land shipping. Columbus wanted to go west and sail around Africa to get to India. He never made it to India. On October 12 of that year, after unknowingly sailing across the Atlantic Ocean, he found himself in the Bahamas, off the coast of what is now called Florida. He had discovered the New World, known today as North and South America. Ironically, the name "America" came from Amerigo Vespucci, another explorer who was the first European to actually discover the mainland that today is called the United States of America.

Different European empires saw an opportunity in the New World to extend their power and build their wealth. The English were the most powerful at the time, and they were determined to settle the new land. In 1607, 100 Englishmen landed off the coast of Virginia and established the first settlement of Jamestown. They were met by natives whom they called Indians, and thus began the sometimes good, sometimes bad relationship that Native Americans would have with their new neighbors.

Despite the difficult living conditions of the New World, many desperate Europeans made the journey across the Atlantic in search of better lives as farmers on land that was plenty and perfect for growing things like tobacco, beans, squash, and tomatoes.

In 1619, the first African slaves were brought to America to work on the large plantations that the Englishmen had established. Over the next 200 years, well over half a million African slaves would be brought over on ships to work and die for white masters who bought them at auctions similar to those that we now have for automobiles. A great number of these slaves, having come from Africa, were Muslim. Despite the conversion of most to Christianity, many continued to practice their faith and traditions well into the 1840s.

British Colonialism

Eventually, the diverse group of settlers and slaves would inhabit newly established colonies all along the Atlantic Coast, and all under the control of the Royal Crown in Great Britain. The British had succeeded in establishing 32 colonies from Canada in the north to Florida in the south, but there were 13 main colonies that would eventually become the original states of the United States of America. They were, in the order of their founding: Virginia, New Hampshire, Massachusetts, Maryland, Connecticut, Rhode Island, North Carolina, New York, New Jersey, Carolina, Pennsylvania, Delaware, and Georgia. These colonies were part of the British Empire, yet they still had their own local governments to handle their day-to-day business activities.

The Americans were, for the most part, loyal to the Crown, and they even fought with the British army to expel the French from the New World. Still they were different--a mixture of English, German, Dutch, Welsh, Scottish, and French--practicing different forms of the same Christian faith. By 1775, there were approximately 2,000 Jews in the colonies. Other than the African slaves, there were only a handful of Muslims at best in America.

The British Parliament imposed a series of taxes on the colonies that angered the Americans. They were upset because these taxes were placed only on Americans and not on the entire empire, and thus the Americans felt that they should not pay such taxes to a government in which they did not have any representatives. There were no Americans in the British Parliament. The Americans resisted the taxes under the slogan, "No Taxation Without Representation!"

Boston, Massachusetts, was the site of many revolts. One ended in the massacre by the British Redcoats (soldiers who wore red coats) of several civilians. Another revolt against a tax on tea led to the "Boston Tea Party," where several men boarded ships that carried tea from the British East India Company and dumped 342 chests of tea into Boston Harbor.

Parliament reacted by cracking down on rebellious colonists and by passing laws that made life more miserable for the Americans, particularly in Massachusetts.

Independence

As tensions continued to rise, the colonists held a first-ever Continental Congress in Philadelphia in 1774 where 12 of the 13 colonies sent representatives to meet and discuss their problems with Parliament. Independence was not on the agenda as of yet. The goal was to return life back to normal as it was before Parliament started collecting special taxes. At the end of the Congress, petitions were approved to be sent to Parliament. A document called "The Association" was signed, putting a complete ban on all the importation and consumption of British goods and the exportation of American goods to Great Britain. Violators of The Association were soaked in hot tar and then covered with chicken feathers and humiliated in front of their neighbors.

The British were very upset and worried about the colonists' rebellion. In April 1775, Redcoats were sent to seize gun powder that was stored in Lexington, Massachusetts, by a colonial militia and to arrest the militia's leaders. A battle broke out that spread to Concord, Massachusetts, where the colonists defeated the Redcoats in the first battle of the Revolutionary War, killing 70 and injuring hundreds more.

In May, the Second Continental Congress was held and the colonists established their own governmental systems, including a postal system, a navy, marine corps, and a foreign bureau to look for help overseas against the British. They were preparing for war.

At this time there were a total of 2.5 million colonists in America, and their new army consisted of poorly trained militiamen who left their farms to fight for freedom. Not all Americans were rebels. The British enlisted 50,000 loyal colonists, or Loyalists, to join them in their war against their revolting countrymen, known as the Patriots. The Revolutionaries were weak militarily, but they were determined to fight for their rights. Patrick Henry, one of the colonial leaders, spoke for all of the Patriots when he wrote, "Give me liberty or give me death."

On July 4, 1776, the Second Continental Congress approved the famous Declaration of Independence, a document that was written mainly by Thomas Jefferson. One of the better-known passages of the document reads

We hold these truths to be self-evident; that all men are created equal; that they are endowed by their Creator with certain inalienable rights; that among these are life, liberty, and the pursuit of happiness.

The United States of America was born, with a government of the people, by the people, and for the people. The power of government was put into the hands of the people.

The declaration did not end the war, which lasted for another seven years. It was expanded into a larger war when the French sent soldiers and ships to assist the Americans in defeating the British, their longtime enemies.

After being humiliated by the Americans, Britain signed a treaty with her former colonies and recognized the independence of the United States of America on larger territory with new borders that went north to the border of Canada, west to the Mississippi River, and south to Florida.

DID YOU KNOW?

During the revolutionary war, there were more American Loyalists who joined the British army to fight the rebels than there were Americans who joined the Patriot army. Also, at the final battle of the war, which took place at Yorktown, Virginia, there were three times as many French soldiers and sailors (29,000) fighting against the British than there were American soldiers and militiamen (11,000).

CHAPTER 2

THE UNITED STATES CONSTITUTION

Shortly before the Declaration of Independence, the Continental Congress established a committee to write a constitution for the new nation that would be born, based on the system of confederation, in which the 13 independent states were loosely joined through a central government. The final product was the Articles of Confederation. This document created a central governmental body, known as the Confederation Congress, in Philadelphia, with the authority to declare war, manufacture money, maintain the postal system, and borrow money. The confederation of states made its central government very weak to protect individual state rights. Although the Articles of Confederation were adopted on November 15, 1777, they did not become law until March 1, 1781.

Each state had one vote in this Congress, which meant that small states with half or even one-quarter the population of larger states had the same power in Congress. There were no executive or judicial branches. Congress could not raise taxes, and it could not control trade, neither among states nor with other nations. Congress could not even have its own central army.

America went through very difficult times in its early years, and the power of government was tested over and over again.

In the end, the Articles of Confederation did not do the job that was needed. In 1786, the states held the Constitutional Convention to discuss changing the Articles, but they quickly moved towards a new model of government that would strengthen the central government, and yet preserve the individual rights of the states. After much debate and compromise, a solution was reached. The Articles of Confederation collapsed as 11 states left Congress. Nine of those 11 voted in favor of a new constitution. This was based on the republican form of government and was implemented through the system of Federalism, with a bicameral (two-house) legislature consisting of the House of Representatives and the Senate.

Key Concepts of the Constitution

The Constitution provides our country with a foundation for government and governing. It is the ultimate law of the land. However, states have their own constitutions, in addition to the federal constitution, in order to exercise their independent powers. The preamble, or introduction, of the U.S. Constitution reads:

> *We the people of the United States, in order to form a more perfect union, establish justice, insure domestic tranquility, provide for the common defense, promote the general welfare, and secure the blessings of liberty to ourselves and our posterity, do ordain and establish this Constitution for the United States of America.*

There are three central concepts to the Constitution:

1. Republican form of government – The United States is a republic in which the people have the ultimate

18

power, and that power is exercised by those that they elect to represent them in government.

2. Organization of government – Government is divided into three parts: legislative (Congress), executive (president), and judicial (courts). The legislative branch makes the laws, the executive branch makes sure the laws are carried out, and the judicial branch interprets the law. The separate function of these three branches is known as the **Separation of Powers**. To make sure that no one branch of government gains more power over the others, there is a system in place known as **Checks and Balances**. For example, Congress may pass a law, but the president may veto it. Still, Congress can override the president's veto with enough votes, but then the Supreme Court may find that the law is unconstitutional, at which point it is no longer a law (*See Figure 1 on page 43*).

3. Federalism – Power is divided between the national government and the states. Some of these powers are specific, and others are very vague and open to debate. However, the federal, or national, government has much more power than the states.

Articles

There are seven main articles of the Constitution, each with its own sections and clauses. The following is a summary of the articles:

Article I   Gives the two-house Congress the power to make laws to collect taxes, borrow money, control foreign and interstate trade, pass naturalization and bankruptcy laws, produce, or coin money, punish counterfeiters, establish a postal service, issue patents and copyrights, establish inferior courts below the Supreme Court, punish crimes committed on the high seas, declare war, maintain and regulate an army and a navy, call out the state militia, share control of militias with states, make laws for the District of Columbia (Washington, DC) and other federal areas. In addition to these specific enumerated powers, Congress has certain implied powers to make laws that it feels are necessary to carry out the enumerated powers mentioned above. Powers that are denied to Congress are: control of the slave trade (decision postponed until 1808), suspending the Writ of Habeas Corpus except during times of rebellion or invasion, passing Ex Post Facto laws, imposing taxes that are not proportionate to population, collect taxes on exports, discrimination against states, spending public money without it being appropriated by Congress through legislation, granting titles of nobility or accepting of gifts from foreign states without congressional approval.

Article II   Gives executive power to the president of the United States of America. Powers given to the president are: the role as commander-in-chief of the armed forces and state militias, to grant reprieves and pardons for those who have committed offenses against the law, except those who were impeached by Congress, to negotiate treaties with foreign nations with the Senate's approval, to appoint ambassadors, Cabinet members, consuls, federal judges, and all other officers of the United States, with the approval of the Senate, to directly appoint officials while the Senate may be in recess, to give Congress a yearly report known as the State of the Union, to convene or adjourn Congress.

Article III   Gives judicial power to the federal courts. It established one Supreme Court, and allows Congress to establish other federal lower courts. Courts shall hear all cases of law and equity arising from the Constitution, laws of the United States, and treaties that the United States has made with foreign bodies. All criminal trials, except in the case of impeachment, shall be by a jury in the state where the crime was committed. This article also provides for the terms in which a person may be tried with treason: if he/she wages war against the U.S., or gives aid and comfort to the enemies of the U.S., and either the testimony of two witnesses who participated in the treason, or an open confession in court will be acceptable. Congress alone shall declare the punishment of treason.

Article IV   Discusses the relationship between states. Includes the Full Faith In Credit clause, which requires states to recognize the public acts, records, and judicial proceedings of every other state in the union. For example, a marriage license issued to a couple in Missouri must be honored by the authorities in Ohio. This article also says that citizenship in one state is valid in any other state and that citizens have the same rights wherever they go, fugitives from justice must be surrendered by the state in which they have fled, runaway slaves must be returned to their masters, new states may be admitted into the union by Congress, all non-state territories will be controlled by Congress, guarantees states' representation in the federal government and protection against invasion or rebellion.

Article V   Allows for the Constitution to be amended (changed). Amendments can be offered by a national convention being called by two-thirds of state legislatures, or by a two-thirds vote in both houses of Congress. At least three-fourths of the 50 states must ratify (vote in favor of) amendments before the Constitution is changed.

Article VI   Offers three general provisions: 1) All debts that the Confederation owed before the Constitution are the responsibility of the United States government; 2) The supreme laws of the land are the Constitution, federal laws, and treaties; 3) All federal and state legislators, judges, and executive officers must take an oath (promise) to support the Constitution when taking office, and that oath cannot include any kind of qualifying test based on religion.

Article VII States that this Constitution will become official once at least 9 of the original 13 states ratify the document. This happened on September 17, 1787.

The federalists who supported the Constitution won a big victory, but the anti-federalists were upset because they feared that the Constitution did not offer individuals any protection from the government. James Madison, a leading federalist who would later become president, prepared a list of amendments, presented them to Congress, and helped secure the two-thirds vote that was needed in Congress in order for the amendments to be voted on by the states. In September 1791, the first 10 amendments to the Constitution were adopted. Because of the protection that was given to citizens, the amendments were called "The Bill of Rights."

The Bill of Rights

1st Amendment   Congress cannot pass a law in favor of one religion, nor can it prohibit people from freely practicing their religion of choice. Congress cannot prevent citizens' freedom of speech, or the freedom of the press to report. People have the right to peacefully assemble (gather), and they have the right to petition the government.

2nd Amendment   Since a well-regulated militia is necessary for the security of the state, the right of the people to keep and bear arms (own weapons) shall not be infringed.

3rd Amendment   People cannot be forced to give soldiers quarters (a room in their home and food), except during war, and in a way that is established by law.

4th Amendment   People, their homes, and possessions are protected from unreasonable searches and seizures. Search warrants must be issued only when there is probable cause (good reason), must usually, but not always, be signed by a judge, and must state specifically the place to be searched, and the possessions or persons to be seized.

5th Amendment   Guarantees the right to life, liberty, and property. A person charged with a crime has the right to refuse to testify against him/herself, and that while accused, that person will receive the full and fair due process of law. A person cannot be put on trial twice for the same crime, or be put into what is known as **Double Jeopardy** (has nothing to do with the game show). Also, the government cannot take someone's property without giving them fair compensation.

6th Amendment   All accused individuals have the right to a fair and speedy public trial, by an impartial jury of fellow citizens in the state where the crime was committed. The accused has the right to see the evidence presented, and know who the witnesses are that testify against him. He has the right to a lawyer, and the right to force people, through subpoenas to testify during the trial.

7th Amendment The rules of common law are recognized for civil (non-criminal) cases, and most cases will be tried by jury.

8th Amendment Cruel and unusual punishment for crimes are prohibited. Also, judges may not set bail so excessive (high) that it is unreasonable, nor may excessive fines be imposed on people who violate the law.

9th Amendment Any other rights not stated in the Constitution are retained by the people.

10th Amendment The powers not given to the federal government through the Constitution are reserved by the state and the people.

Since the passage of the Bill of Rights over 200 years ago, there have only been 17 amendments made to the Constitution, bringing the total to 27. Each amendment has an important historical significance and allows insight into the mood of American politics at the time of its passage. The 13th, 14th, and 15th Amendments, all passed between 1865 and 1870, ended slavery, gave all U.S. citizens equal protection under the law, and gave all eligible people the right to vote, respectively. At that time though, those who were eligible to vote were only male adults. Not until the 19th Amendment was passed in 1920 did women get the right to vote in the United States. In 1971, the 26th Amendment set the minimum voting age at 18 for all Americans.

DID YOU KNOW?

The 18th Amendment, passed in 1919, outlawed the sale of alcohol across the United States. Known as Prohibition, it was later repealed in 1933 by the 21st Amendment.

CHAPTER 3

THE CONGRESS

The responsibility of making laws and of overseeing departments and agencies that implement those laws is what the legislative body of the federal government does. Congress carries this responsibility. It is a bicameral body, which means that it has two chambers: the Senate and the House of Representatives (the House).

The House

Members of the House are known as representatives or congressmen. Those elected to serve in the House must be at least 25 years old and must have been a citizen of the U.S. for at least 7 years. Since 1929, the number of representatives in the House has been set at 435. Each member represents a congressional district of approximately 600,000 people. States like California (53), New York (29), and Illinois (19) have a large number of congressional districts, while others like Hawaii (2), Delaware (1), and Montana (1) have very few. Since the District of Columbia (Washington, DC) is a city that is not part of any state, it does not have a representative. Instead, it has what is called a **Delegate**. In addition to the congressional districts within the United States, there are territories under U.S. control like American Samoa,

Guam, Puerto Rico and the U.S. Virgin Islands that have delegates in Congress. The delegates from the District of Columbia and the other U.S. territories have the same voting rights as other members in their committees, but they do not have the right to vote when the entire House is in session and making final decisions on legislation.

Members of the House are elected every two years. The framers of the Constitution thought that allowing the people to directly elect their representatives for short terms would ensure that the people were truly being represented in Washington. If the constituents (citizens of a district) do not like the job that their representative is doing, they may vote for someone else in the next election. Therefore, if a congressman wants to stay in office, he will work hard to please his constituency and fight for their interests.

Although they are not required to be affiliated with a political party, representatives are usually members of the Democratic or Republican Party. They may, however, affiliate themselves with other small parties, or classify themselves as independent.

Structure

The party that has a majority of seats in the House (218 or more) picks the **Speaker of the House** as the leader of the entire chamber. The speaker is the most powerful person in Congress. He is the next person in line to take over if something happens to the president and vice president. Assisting the speaker is the **Majority Leader**, who is from the speaker's party, and is elected only by the party caucus (all members of that party). The **Minority Leader** heads the other political party in the House. To assist the majority and minority leaders, both caucuses separately elect a **Whip**. It is the whip's job to make sure that party members vote a certain way on bills, and to keep them informed about legislation, schedules, and other things. Table 1 shows the House leadership for 2003 - 2004.

Table 1: The House Leadership for the 108th Congress (2003-2004)

• House Speaker	J. Dennis Hastert (R-IL)*
• Majority Leader	Tom DeLay (R-TX)
• Minority Leader	Nancy Pelosi (D-CA)*
• Majority Whip	Roy Blunt (R-MO)
• Minority Whip	Steny H. Hoyer (D-MD)

* R=Republican, D=Democrat

Most of the work done in Congress happens in committees. These committees are specialized to deal with legislation on certain topics. Committees break down further into subcommittees to deal with more specific aspects of the committee's issue area. There are four types of committees: 1) Standing Committee-permanent committees that determine whether pieces of legislation should be passed on to the full chamber for a vote; 2) Select Committee–temporary committee to examine issues of great importance to society; 3) Conference Committee-a committee formed by members of the House and Senate to negotiate for one version of two similar bills passed separately in each chamber; 4) Joint Committee-committees formed by House and Senate members to examine certain issues, with the leadership rotating back and forth between the members of both chambers.

The House has many powers that the Senate does not. Revenue (tax) and appropriation (spending) bills can only originate in the House. Also, only the House can draw up

Table 2: House Committees and Subcommittees of the 108th Congress (2003-2004)

COMMITTEE	SUBCOMMITTEES
Agriculture	Conservation, Credit, Rural Development and Research. Dept Operations, Oversight, Nutrition & Forestry. General Farm Commodities & Risk Management. Livestock & Horticulture. Specialty Crops & Foreign Agriculture Programs.
Appropriations Approves spending for departments and programs	Agriculture, Rural Development, Food and Drug Administration & Related Agencies. Commerce, Justice, State, & Judiciary. Defense. District of Columbia. Energy & Water Development. Foreign Operations, Export Financing, and Related Programs. Interior. Labor, Health and Human Services and Education. Legislative. Military Construction. Transportation. Treasury, Postal Service & General Government. Veterans Affairs, Housing and Urban Development, and Independent Agencies. Homeland Security.
Armed Services	Tactical Air and Land Forces. Readiness. Terrorism, Unconvential Threats and Capabilities. Total Force. Strategic Forces. Projection Forces.
Budget	None
Education and Workforce	Education Reform. Employer-Employee Relations. Select Education. 21st Century Competitiveness. Workforce Protection.
Energy and Commerce	Commerce, Trade and Consumer Protection. Energy and Air Quality. Environment and Hazardous Materials. Health. Oversight and Investigation. Telecommunications and the Internet.
Financial Services	Capital Markets, Insurance, and Government Sponsored Enterprise. Domestic and International Monetary Policy Trade and Technology. . Financial Institutions and Consumer Credit. Housing and Community Opportunity. Oversight and Investigation.
Government Reform	Civil Service and Agency Organization. Criminal Justice, Drug Policy, and Human Resources. Energy Policy, Natural Resources and Regulatory Affairs. National Security, Emerging Threats and International Relations. Human Rights and Wellness. Government Efficiency and Financial Management. Technology, Information Policy, Intergovernmental Relations and the Census.
House Administration	None
International Relations	Africa. Asia, the Pacific. Europe. International Terrorism, Nonproliferation & Human Rights. Middle East & Central Asia. Western Hemisphere.
Judiciary	Commercial and Administrative Law. Courts, the Internet, and Intellectual Property. Crime. Immigration, Border Security and Claims. The Constitution. Crime, Terrorism and Homeland Security.
Resources	Energy and Mineral Resources. Fisheries Conservation, Wildlife and Oceans. Forests and Forest Health. National Parks, Recreation and Public Lands. Water and Power.
Rules	Legislative and Budget Process. Technology and the House.
Science	Energy. Environment, Technology & Standards. Research. Space & Aeronautics.
Small Business	Regulatory Reform and Oversight. Technology, Rural Enterprises and Agricultural Policy. Tax, Finance, and Exports. Workforce Empowerment, and Government Programs
Standards of Official Conduct	None
Transportation and Infrastructure	Aviation. Coast Guard and Maritime Transportation. Economic Development, Public Buildings and Emergency Management. Highways, Pipelines and Transit. Railroads. Water Resources and Environment.
Veterans Affairs	Benefits. Health. Oversight and Investigation.
Ways and Means	Health. Human Resources. Oversight. Select Revenue Measures. Social Security. Trade.
Permanent Select Committee on Intelligence	Human Intelligence, Analysis & Counterintelligence. Intelligence Policy & National Security. Technical & Tactical Intelligence. Terrorism and Homeland Security.
Select Committee on Homeland Security	Infrastructure and Border Security. Rules. Emergency Preparedness and Response. Cybersecurity, Science, and Research & Development. Intelligence and Counterterrorism.

Shaded areas represent Committees most important to Muslims

articles of impeachment in order to remove from office the president, vice president, or federal judges.

Of most interest to Muslims are the International Relations Committee, the Select Committee on Homeland Security, the Appropriations Committee, and the Judiciary Committee (*see Table 2*). The International Relations Committee is where legislation regarding foreign policy is considered. The most zealous supporters of Israel sit on this committee. The Appropriations Committee is important because this is where all funding for foreign aid is approved in the House. Israel would not get billions of dollars a year in aid if the Appropriations Committee did not approve it. The Judiciary Committee is very important because of the issues of civil rights and immigration. The Homeland Security Committee will oversee how the war on terror is conducted, and that will undoubtedly have an impact on the lives of Muslim-Americans.

The **Chairman** of a committee is always from the majority party, and is usually, but not always, the longest serving majority member in that committee. Each party caucus in the House assigns its members to various committees, no more than two per member. The House leadership, however, has a great deal of influence in the selection of chairmen and the committee assignments. An example is the International Relations Committee chaired by Henry Hyde (R-IL). That committee has 26 Republicans and 23 Democrats. Since votes in committee need a simple majority (50%) to pass, the Republicans will always win if they vote together. If at least 25 Republicans vote for something, it will pass, or if they vote against something, it will fail, guaranteed, no matter how many Democrats voted for or against the issue. The

Ethics Committee is the only one with half of its members from the majority and half from the minority.

The person who leads the minority party in the committee and subcommittee is known as the **Ranking Member**. This leadership position is also based on seniority. The chairman and the ranking member work together to make sure that committee business runs as smoothly as possible. Sometimes that is not possible at all.

The Senate

Members of the Senate are simply known as senators. Senators must be at least 30 years old and have been U.S. citizens for at least 9 years. There are 100 senators in this senior and more prestigious chamber. Each state, regardless of population, elects two senators to each serve six-year terms. The framers of the Constitution wanted senators, unlike their colleagues in the House, not to be controlled by public opinion, which is often changing. The Senate is meant to consider the long-term effects of public policy and legislation. Originally, senators were chosen by the legislatures in their state, not by the people. The direct election of senators by the people became law in 1913 after the 17th Amendment was passed. Whereas the entire House is up for election every two years, only one-third of the Senate is up for election every two years.

Structure

The leadership structure within the Senate itself is a little different than that of the House. The Senate has both majority and minority leaders, as well as whips. Senate committees and subcommittees follow the same leadership model as the

House. Officially, the **Vice President** is the **President of the Senate**. In reality, the vice president almost never appears in the Senate. He will usually appear if there is a 50/50 tie on a vote. His vote will break that tie. Therefore the day-to-day presiding officer in the Senate is the **President Pro Tempore**. Again, this position is usually honorary and is given to the longest serving senator on the majority side. The President Pro Tempore during the 108th Congress was Ted Stevens (R-AL), who has been serving in the Senate since 1968. The real work in the Senate is done by several senators. The majority leader is the most powerful among them since he has the power of the majority behind him to set the Senate's agenda.

Individually, senators have much more power than congressmen. There is usually no time limit set when a senator speaks on the floor of the Senate. If he wishes, he may speak for as long as he wants, on any subject he desires, creating what is called a filibuster. He will do this to protest something and stop any other activity on the Senate floor. Once, a Senator began reading names from a phonebook just to waste time and frustrate his opponents. A filibuster can only be defeated when 16 members sign a petition, and then 60 senators vote in favor of a motion called a cloture in order to stop the filibuster.

Just as in the House, the Senate Judiciary, Appropriations, and Foreign Relations Committees have a profound impact on Muslim lives (*see Table 3*). Because of the enormous power of the Senate and the relatively small number of its members, the pro-Israel lobby has focused much of its energy on maintaining strong support for Israel in the Senate. An example of this power is when the American-Israel Public Affairs Committee (AIPAC) seeks signatures for a letter to be sent to

Table 3: Senate Committees & Subcommittees of the 108th Congress (2003-2004)

COMMITTEE	SUBCOMMITTEES
Agriculture, Nutrition and Forestry	Forestry, Conservation, and Rural Revitalization. Marketing, Inspection, and Product Promotion. Production and Price Competitiveness. Research, Nutrition, and General Legislation.
Appropriations	Agriculture, Rural Development, and Related Agencies. Commerce, Justice, State, and Judiciary. Defense. District of Columbia. Energy and Water Development. Foreign Operations. Interior. Labor, Health and Human Services, Education. Legislative Branch. Military Construction. Transportation, Treasury and General Government. Veterans Affairs, Housing and Urban Development, and Independent Agencies. Homeland Security.
Armed Services	Airland. Emerging Threats and Capabilities. Personnel. Readiness and Management Support. Sea Power. Strategic Forces.
Banking, Housing and Urban Affairs	Economic Policy. Financial Institutions. Housing, and Transportation. International Trade and Finance. Securities and Investment.
Budget	None
Commerce, Science and Transportation	Aviation. Communications. Coast Guard, Oceans and Fisheries. Science, Technology, and Space. Surface Transportation and Merchant Marine. Competition, Foreign Commerce and Infrastructure. Consumer Affairs and Product Safety.
Energy and Natural Resources	Energy National Parks. Water and Power. Public Lands and Forests.
Environment and Public Works	Clean Air, Climate Change and Nuclear Safety. Fisheries, Wildlife and Water. Superfund, Waste Management. Transportation and Infrastructure.
Finance	Health Care. International Trade. Long-Term Growth and Debt Reduction. Social Security and Family Policy. Taxation and IRS Oversight.
Foreign Relations	African Affairs. East Asian and Pacific Affairs. European Affairs. International Economic Policy, Export and Trade Promotion. International Operations and Terrorism. Near Eastern and South Asian Affairs. Western Hemisphere, Peace Corp, Narcotics Affairs.
Government Affairs	Financial Management, the Budget, and International Security. Oversight of Government Management, The Federal Workforce, and the District of Columbia. Permanent Subcommittee on Investigations.
Health, Education, Labor and Pensions	Aging. Children and Families. Employment, Safety, and Training. Substance Abuse and Mental Health Services.
Judiciary	Administrative Oversight and the Courts. Antitrust, Competition and Consumer Rights. The Constitution. Civil Rights and Property Rights. Crime, Corrections and Victims Rights. Immigration, Border Security and Citizenship. Terrorism, Technology and Homeland Security.
Rules and Administration	None
Small Business and Entrepreneurship	None
Veterans' Affairs	None
Indian Affairs	None
Select Committee on Ethics	None
Select Committee on Intelligence	None
Special Committee on Aging	None

Shaded areas represent committees most important to Muslims

34

the president that condemns the Palestinians and praises Israel. In 2001, 89 out of the 100 senators signed such a letter.

Like the House, the Senate has its own unique powers. Whereas the House may impeach an official, the Senate holds the trial, and its members become the jury, and the **Chief Justice** of the Supreme Court resides as the judge. The Senate must approve all of those who are nominated by the president to serve as ambassadors, Cabinet members, or other high-level officials. The Senate must also approve foreign treaties negotiated by the president before the United States officially signs on.

Congressional Offices

Each member of Congress has at least one office on Capitol Hill--the campus that houses the Capitol building where the House and Senate chambers are and several office buildings. Legislators have offices in their home district or state as well. Congressmen may have a main district office with one or more smaller satellite offices. Senators have many regional offices all across the state, with the headquarters either in the state capital or in the largest city in the state. Some explanation of the word capital is important here. The word capital (with "al") refers to the city where the governmental headquarters of a state or country are housed. The word Capitol (with "ol") refers only to the place where Congress, or a state legislature, is housed. So Congress is housed on Capitol Hill in the capital of the United States, Washington, DC.

Congressmen and senators would not be able to do their job if not for the help of their staff, both in DC and in the home district or state. The staff works on legislative issues by

35

researching and writing. It also handles constituent services, such as arranging tours of the Capitol and the White House for constituents who visit DC, handling orders from constituents who wish to pay for a flag that is flown over the Capitol, investigating problems that constituents are having with governmental departments or agencies, and helping to get funding for community projects. Each member of Congress has a budget for the hiring of staff and for office expenses. Congressional offices will have between 5 and 10 staffers in DC, and almost an equal number in their districts. Senators have much larger staffs of anywhere from 15 to 50 persons both in DC and in the state offices. The professional staff is not allowed to do any campaign work while at the office or while working on official time. The employees that handle campaigns are usually separate from the professional staff, although many staffers volunteer time after hours to work on campaigns.

The following is a list of the major staff positions in a congressional office as well as their major tasks:

Administrative Assistant (AA)-More commonly known as the **Chief of Staff**, this person runs the office operations in general and oversees the work of other staffers. The AA is also responsible for calculating the political risks and benefits of legislation and maintaining good relations between the office and the constituents.

Legislative Director (LD)-This person is responsible for all legislation that originates out of that member's office, and for keeping the member informed about scheduling of legislative action. The LD advises the member on other pieces of legislation that are being considered.

Legislative Assistant (LA)-The LA assists the LD by working on designated issue areas. The LA's focus is on understanding these issues, researching bills related to his/her area of expertise, and working with outside groups and agencies to get input.

Press Secretary/Communications Director-All requests for interviews and information from the media go through this person. This staffer also maintains contacts with journalists and community leaders in order to make sure that the member's point of view on issues is getting across clearly. Press releases, press conferences, newsletters, and perhaps even website maintenance are all responsibilities of this person. Many offices have assistant press secretaries to help with this sometimes overwhelming position.

Scheduler-This person is the one who makes all appointments for the member. From floor debates to community town hall meetings, the scheduler puts it all together and informs the member of appointments.

Caseworker-The caseworker handles complaints by constituents about poor service from governmental agencies and helps with other problems that they may be having. The caseworker investigates the complaint and tries to help solve the problem. If a problem is very serious, the caseworker may inform the member about the situation.

Knowing who's who in a congressional office is critical for people who want to lobby members on issues that are important to them. If someone wants the member to speak at a community function, he would call the scheduler directly. If someone had a concern with U.S. policy in some part of the world, he would call and speak with the LA that handles foreign affairs. If someone has a problem getting their social security check, he should call and speak to a caseworker. It is not necessary to always speak to the member, nor is it likely that the member will always meet with those who wish to meet with him/her. The staff advises the member, so if one can convince the staffer that the member should support a certain position, then that makes the likelihood of success much greater (Lobbying will be discussed in detail later in the book in chapters 9 and 10).

How A Bill Becomes Law

Laws are made in Congress for the benefit of the people and the nation, or at least that is the intention. In Congress, potential laws are introduced, debated, changed, and then either rejected or approved for presidential action. The majority of these proposals originate in the House, so the process of lawmaking in that body will be the main focus of this section.

There are four types of proposals, or pieces of legislation that members of the House or Senate may introduce: a bill, a joint resolution, a concurrent resolution, and a simple resolution. Bills are the most common form of legislation, usually to make new laws, change old ones, approve spending, and impose taxes. Joint resolutions can be introduced in either of the chambers. The word "joint" does not mean that the exact same resolution has been submitted in both chambers at the same time. Actually, there is not much of a difference between bills and joint resolutions. Bills that are later amended are done so through joint resolutions, and joint resolutions that may later be changed are amended through bills. Concurrent and simple resolutions are very different from bills and joint resolutions because they deal with the internal business of Congress, not laws, and therefore, do not go to the president for approval. The concurrent resolution may be introduced in either chamber and will usually express the feelings and opinion of the Congress on certain issues. The simple resolution is something done individually for each chamber only. The House may vote in favor of a simple resolution that expresses support for the president during a time of war. This action stays in the House, and is not sent to the Senate nor the president for their approval. For practical purposes, all legislation will be referred to as "bills" from here on out.

Members of the House introduce bills for many reasons. During every congressional cycle (2 years), approximately 10,000 pieces of legislation are introduced, but only about 400 will ever pass the entire House. Some bills may pass through Congress quickly, while others may go through a long process of hearings and debate. Most bills are never considered and eventually die. Whether a bill lives or dies depends on politics and public opinion.

The president of the United States has a legislative agenda that he presents to Congress during his State of the Union address every winter. When major legislation is drafted by the White House, it is sent to the speaker and the president of the Senate. They will in turn send that draft to the appropriate committee. The chairman and/or ranking member of the committee will then introduce the draft as a bill. This process is known as Executive Communication.

A congressman may see the need for a new law, or may feel that an existing law needs to be changed. He may get these ideas from his staff, constituents, or interest groups. He will take this idea and then present it to a member of the House Legislative Counsel, a group of legislative experts who will tell him if and how his idea can be turned into a valid bill. Once legislative counsel edits the bill and approves it for introduction, the congressman will take the bill, which may be 1 page or 100 pages, inside the House chambers where he will then put it in the "hopper," a box that the **House Clerk** uses to collect bills and other items. The clerk will assign the bill a number, and then the speaker will forward the bill to the committee that deals with the issue discussed in the bill. The speaker may send different parts of a large bill to different committees for considerations, while assigning one committee as the primary committee with authority over the entire bill. Committees in turn send bills down to the proper subcommittee for hearings and investigations.

The most critical phase of the process for a bill is when it is in committee. The first thing that the subcommittee may do is to get the input of the government department or agency that deals with the topic addressed by the bill. Then hearings may be scheduled in the subcommittee for government officials, experts, lobbyists, and citizens to express their support of or opposition to the bill, and why. During the hearings, members ask the witnesses who are testifying questions after the witnesses read a summary of their written statement that is submitted to the committee.

After hearings are complete, the subcommittee will schedule a "mark-up," or a meeting to vote on the bill. The result of the vote is reported to the full committee. Usually, the committee will accept the recommendation of the subcommittee to approve the bill or kill it. If the committee accepts a favorable recommendation for a bill, it will then debate the bill and allow members to amend it if they desire. Members may intentionally add many amendments to a bill that they want to kill. This is known as "pigeonholing." When debate is over, the committee will vote on the bill with the approved amendments. If a bill passes, a report of that bill is sent on to the Rules Committee where the rules for debate time and amendments will be set. The final product is sent to the speaker, and it is up to him to schedule bills for floor action.

This is where the great power of the speaker is apparent. A bill may go through the whole process mentioned above, and then get stuck on the speaker's desk and eventually die at the end of the congressional term if the speaker decides that he does not want the bill to go to the floor for a vote. There may be political reasons for this as well as pressure from the White House or other members of the congressional leadership who want to kill the bill.

Those bills that are scheduled by the speaker are debated on the House floor for a limited amount of time and then voted on. The process is somewhat different with regards to procedure, debate time, amendments, and voting. This is where politics comes into play. There are different reasons why a legislator votes for or against bills. They may like a bill, but know that their constituents would not like it. Or they may feel that even if a bill is popular with the people, it is bad policy and they will vote against it. Often legislators vote the way the party leadership tells them to vote. This is called "party-line" voting. If the member does not vote with his party, he will be politically punished, and the bills that he has introduced may not get the support of the party. There are countless influences on a member when he is deciding to vote one way or another.

Congressmen and senators may try to kill a bill by attaching amendments that would hurt the chances of that bill being passed. Other members may seek favors for their vote from the sponsor(s) of the bill or the leadership by asking to attach an amendment known as a "rider," which would benefit that member's district or state. Riders are usually associated with larger bills. This phenomenon is known as "pork barrel" politics--everyone gets their share.

A member may vote for someone's bill if it does not affect their district or state and expect the sponsor of that bill to vote for his bills in the future. This is called "log-rolling." In the House, members are more dependent on one another and their party, while senators have much more individual power. As mentioned earlier, a senator can merely filibuster a bill he does not like and stop it from a vote until he is clotured.

When legislation is passed in one chamber, it will then be sent to the other chamber for action. Once both chambers each pass their own versions of a bill, they will hold a Conference Committee to work on creating an identical document that can be presented to the president. If the differences are not worked out, the bill will die. If they are worked out, the identical bill will be sent back to each chamber in a "conference report" where it will be voted on. If the conference report is approved by both chambers, it will then be sent to the White House for the president's signature.

Once the bill reaches the White House, the president has 10 days to sign it into law. The bill will still become law if the president does not sign it after 10 days unless Congress adjourns before the 10 days are up, at which point the bill becomes rejected through what is called a "pocket veto."

If the president does not like the bill, he will veto it and it will go back to Congress where two-thirds of its members would have to vote in favor of the bill to override the president's veto. These overrides are rare, but they are more likely to happen when the president is from one party and both

Figure 1: How a Bill Becomes a Law

HOW A BILL BECOMES A LAW		
BILL INTRODUCED IN HOUSE either chamber or both	⇦ ⇨	**BILL INTRODUCED IN SENATE** either chamber or both
⬇		⬇
BILL ASSIGNED TO COMMITTEE might go to subcommittee		**BILL ASSIGNED TO COMMITTEE** might go to subcommittee
Hearings and Testimony		**Hearings and Testimony**
Markups and Votes		**Markups and Votes**
Reports		**Reports**
⬇		⬇
DEBATE ON HOUSE FLOOR majority vote in favor of bill	⬉ ⬈	**DEBATE ON SENATE FLOOR** majority vote in favor of bill
	⬇	
CONFERENCE COMMITTEE agrees on final joint version to send to the president		
	⬇	
PRESIDENT Signs Bill into Law or Vetoes it		
	⬇	
SUPREME COURT rules on Constitutionality of Law if it is Challenged		

Source: University of Michigan Library

chambers of Congress are controlled by the other party. The president had the power between 1996-1998 to exercise a "line-item" veto where he would only strike down the parts of a bill that he did not like. This process was later determined unconstitutional.

The mere threat of vetoing a bill often forces Congress to abandon their plans for passing that bill.

DID YOU KNOW?

The USA PATRIOT Act, which was passed 44 days after 9/11, has 1,016 sections. The second section of the bill condemns discrimination against Muslim and Arab-Americans:

It is the sense of Congress that--

(1) the civil rights and civil liberties of all Americans, including Arab Americans, Muslim Americans, and Americans from South Asia, must be protected, and that every effort must be taken to preserve their safety.

(2) any acts of violence or discrimination against any Americans be condemned, and

(3) the Nation is called upon to recognize the patriot ism of fellow citizens from all ethnic, racial, and religious backgrounds.

CHAPTER 4

THE PRESIDENCY

The presidency is about much more than just one person. It is a huge institution that continuously tends to the operations of the federal government. The Constitution established the executive branch of the government with the president as the head of that branch. The presidency can be compared with the structure of a large corporation. The president of the United States has a Cabinet, or a board, whose members are the heads of the different departments of the government. Like the CEO of a corporation, the president is responsible for the functions of his business--the government--and he in turn delegates responsibility to those he sees fit to get the job done. The Articles of Confederation did not provide for a president because the early Americans did not want another tyrant like the king of England to rule them. When the framers were drafting the Constitution, they still had a fear of tyranny, but they felt that a strong independent executive branch led by the president would be good for the country, so long as he did not have absolute power.

To be eligible for president, a person must be at least 35 years old and must have been born in the United States. If a person was born to parents who were American citizens living outside of the country at the time of birth, that person is considered a natural citizen and can run for president so long as he/she meets the age requirement and has lived in the United States for at least 14 years.

The president serves a four-year term and may only serve two terms maximum. These terms do not have to be back to back. Grover Cleveland served as president between 1885-1889, lost the next election, ran again and won the presidency in 1893 (*see list of U.S. Presidents in Appendix III*).

Assisting the president is the vice president, who is elected together with the president on one party ticket. By law, the vice president cannot be from the same state as the president. Although Americans vote for the president and vice president, they do not elect them directly. This is done through the electoral college (*see Chapter 8*). The vice president is the President of the Senate officially, but as discussed in Chapter 3, he rarely performs in that capacity. The main task of the vice president is to assist the president in forming and implementing policy. The vice president may be put in charge of a major project that the president is working on, or he may try to gain support for the president's agenda by lobbying members of Congress. The vice president does not have the luxury of having his office in his home like his boss. The vice president lives in Northwest Washington, DC at the official vice presidential residence. His main office is in the Eisenhower Executive Office Building, which is next to the West Wing of the White House. The West Wing is where the president's Oval Office is located.

Presidential Powers and Functions

The president of the United States is not only the most powerful man in the country, he is indeed the most powerful man in the world, as America is the only superpower on the planet. The president negotiates treaties on behalf of the entire nation with other countries. Some treaties may be simple trade treaties dealing with the importation of bananas. Others may be more difficult and serious ones like the nuclear arms treaties signed over the years with the former Soviet Union. These treaties do not become law, however, until two-thirds of the Senate approves them.

At home, the president has the enormous power of appointing hundreds of people to government positions ranging from ambassadors, federal judges, agency directors, and Cabinet members. Most of those nominated for appointment by the president are members of his political party. Many of these nominations are rewards for political support or campaign contributions to the president, while others are nominated strictly based on their qualifications. Although the president has the power to pick whom he wants to work for him, those appointments must be approved by the Senate. Nominees may have a difficult time getting appointed if a party other than the president's controls the Senate.

The executive communication powers of the president were discussed earlier. These are the legislative initiatives that the president wants passed through Congress. As required by the Constitution, the president outlines his agenda during the annual State of the Union address before a joint session of Congress.

The president can pardon people convicted of federal crimes, except impeachment. President Clinton was accused of pardoning several people who did not deserve it in the days and hours before the end of his presidency in 2001. Those complaints did not matter much because he had the power to pardon, and he carried out those powers to his liking.

47

As **Commander in Chief**, the president is the head of all of the nation's armed forces. He is also the only one who can approve a nuclear strike against another nation. Whenever the president leaves the White House, an officer of the military is right by him with a briefcase in hand that has the codes necessary to launch a nuclear attack. Congress can only declare war on another nation, but the president still has the power to send troops to foreign countries for up to 60 days without approval from Congress. By that point, the president must consult with Congress and receive their approval for an extension of the troop deployment if American forces are to stay overseas. Examples of such instances during the Clinton administration are Somalia, Haiti, Bosnia, and Kosovo. After 9/11, tens of thousands of American troops were sent to Afghanistan and Iraq to fight wars in those respective countries. A declaration of war was never made by Congress in any of these cases, but American troops were still actively engaged in these areas for various reasons.

Because of the president's role as commander in chief, the American people prefer to have a president with military experience. This is not absolute, for Bill Clinton never served in the military but he served two terms in office. President George W. Bush served in the Air National Guard during the Vietnam war, but he never served in combat overseas.

As the **Head of State**, the president greets foreign leaders at the White House, throws out the first pitch at the World Series, leads the nation through times of crisis, and represents America on trips abroad. This role is more diplomatic and ceremonial, but it is still important for the image of American democracy abroad, as well as for the image of a true leader at home. Presidents take on special projects that they personally get involved in. For Jimmy Carter and Bill Clinton, this project was the Middle East peace process.

As **Chief Executive**, the president is in charge of all of the departments, agencies, and programs of the government. Again, this goes back to the earlier comparison of the president and the CEO of a corporation. The president sets the broad policies and strategies for the various segments of the bureaucracy. A major part of this function is ensuring that all laws of the land are executed and enforced by the government.

As **Party Leader**, the president leads his political party, and rewards its members with jobs, programs, and policy. Rarely will members of the president's party in Congress go against his proposals. That is like a child disobeying his father. This function is unofficial in the sense that the president does not, for the most part, deal with the inner workings of the party. On the other hand, as the leader of the free world, the president automatically assumes the role as the leader of his own political party.

The Cabinet

The **Cabinet** is made up of the heads of the 15 governmental departments that advise the president on their areas of responsibility (*see Table 4*). These department heads all have the title of **Secretary** (example: Secretary of State), except for the head of the Justice Department, whose title is **Attorney General**. There are also individuals who are Cabinet-rank officials who participate in Cabinet sessions. Those given Cabinet-rank status may vary from one president to another. George W. Bush's Cabinet-rank officials are the vice president, the president's chief of staff, the head of the **Environmental Protection Agency (EPA)**, the director of the

Office of Management and Budget (OMB), the **U.S. Trade Representative**, and the director of the **Office of National Drug Control Policy**.

When a president leaves office, his Cabinet usually leaves with him, making way for a new administration that will appoint people because of their qualifications or simply because of politics. The president makes sure that he surrounds himself with people who are not only competent, but more importantly, loyal.

Table 4: Cabinet of President Bush in 2004

Governmental Departments	Department Head
Agriculture	Secretary Ann M. Venneman
Commerce	Secretary Don Evans
Defense	Secretary Donald Rumsfeld
Education	Secretary Rod Paige
Energy	Secretary Spencer Abraham
Health and Human Services	Secretary Tommy Thompson
Homeland Security	Secretary Tom Ridge
Housing and Urban Development	Secretary Alphonso Jackson
Interior	Secretary Gale Norton
Justice	Attorney General John Ashcroft
Labor	Secretary Elaine Chao
State	Secretary Colin Powell
Transportation	Secretary Norman Mineta
Treasury	Secretary John Snow
Veterans Affairs	Secretary Anthony Principi

Many well-known agencies and bureaus are controlled by these departments, while others are independent. The **Federal Bureau of Investigation (FBI)** and the **Drug Enforcement Agency (DEA)** are both part of the Justice Department. The **Central Intelligence Agency (CIA)** and the **National Security Agency (NSA)** are the nation's most important intelligence gathering bodies, and both are independent of government departments. All government agencies and departments have their own objectives, missions, and agendas, as well as limits that they must stay within. The CIA, for instance, gathers intelligence secretly and openly around the world, and launches many operations for the benefit of the nation. However, they cannot operate within the United States, unless as part of an inter-agency task force, because the FBI has jurisdiction (responsibility within a certain area) over the entire country.

The Homeland Security Act of 2002 brought about the largest government reorganization since World War II. The Act established a new arm of the federal government known as the Department of Homeland Security. The goal was to bring together different government agencies that had responsibility for some aspect of protecting the homeland but were scattered throughout the various departments of the government.

The **U.S. Secret Service**, which was formerly under the Treasury Department, and the **U.S. Coast Guard**, which used to be part of the Department. of Transportation, are now both located within the structure of the Department of Homeland Security. **The Bureau of Citizenship and Immigration Services (BCIS)** has now replaced the Immigration and Naturalization Services (INS), which incidentally used to be part of the Justice Department.

Executive Office of the President

The president has several specialized offices within the **Executive Office of the President (EOP)** to help him make policy decisions and carry out his agenda. The EOP employs some 5,000 people who work in the White House, mainly in the West Wing, the Eisenhower Executive Office Building, and the Old Executive Office Building. The president does not have to worry about driving to work every morning, because his residence is on the third floor of the White House, totally separate from all other areas of the building.

One of the more important offices within the EOP is the **National Security Council (NSC)**, which includes the president, vice president, heads of intelligence, and military officials. The **National Security Advisor** runs the NSC.

One of the newest offices within the EOP is the **Office of Faith-Based and Community Initiatives**. This office is designed to help religious institutions and community groups who provide social services get government funding.

Mosques that provide day-care or feed the homeless can get in touch with this office to see if they qualify for government assistance. Many Muslim leaders were happy to see this initiative because they felt that it would mean an expansion of existing services, as well as the establishment of new projects by mosques and other Muslim institutions. Other leaders were cautious, fearing that the initiative would only help Christian Evangelical groups, the conservative core of the president's Republican party.

Presidential Succession

One of the obvious needs for a vice president is for the ability of the government to continue to function in the event that the president dies or is unable to perform his duties due to illness. This concept is known as the **Continuity of Government.** In times of crisis, as on 9/11, the Secret Service immediately separates the president and vice president so that if there was an attack at their location, at least one of them would survive in order to lead the nation.

Who will succeed if something happens to both the president and vice president? The Constitution answers this question with the rules for **Presidential Succession.** This chain of succession is as follows: *President→Vice President→Speaker of the House→Senate President Pro Tempore→Secretary of State→Secretary of Defense→etc.* The list goes on through the remaining members of the Cabinet. Such scenarios seem impossible, but this system has been put in place in the darkest event that so many government officials would be killed by an attack. When the president gives his State of the Union speech before a joint session of Congress every year, all of the members of the Cabinet are present except for one. That one is hidden somewhere in case of an attack on the Capitol that kills all of the other officials. This would ensure the continuity of government.

Examples of succession are as follows. In 1841 President William Henry Harrison died of pneumonia after serving only 31 days in office. He was succeeded by his vice president John Tyler. In 1865, at the end of a bitter civil war that tore this country apart, President Abraham Lincoln was assassinated by John Wilkes Booth at the Ford's Theatre in Washington, DC, as the president was enjoying the play *Our American Cousin.* Lincoln was succeeded by Vice President Andrew Johnson. Nearly 100 years later in 1963, President John F. Kennedy was assassinated in Dallas by Lee Harvey Oswald. Ironically, like Lincoln, Kennedy was succeeded by his vice president whose last name was also Johnson, Lyndon B. Johnson. A more controversial succession took place in 1974 when President Richard M. Nixon resigned from office over a criminal scandal known as Watergate. Nixon's vice president, Gerald Ford, took office and pardoned Nixon of any wrongdoing before Congress had the chance to impeach him.

DID YOU KNOW?

President George Washington (1789-1797) turned down an offer from his army officers to make him the king of the United States after winning independence from the British.

President John Quincy Adams (1825-1829) was elected to the House of Representatives AFTER he left the White House in 1829. He served in the House from 1831 until his death in 1848.

President Abraham Lincoln (1861-1865) often carried letters, bills, and other papers in his tall black stovepipe hat.

President William Taft (1909-1913) weighed more than 300 pounds and had a special oversized bathtub installed for him in the White House.

President Gerald Ford (1974-1977) turned down offers to play professional football with the Green Bay Packers and the Detroit Lions.

President Ronald Reagan (1981-1989) was a lifeguard at Riverside Beach near Dixon, IL, when he was in high school. He rescued 77 people from drowning. Also, before becoming the 40th president of the United States, Reagan was a famous Hollywood actor, and he served as governor of California, just like Arnold Schwarzenegger.

Source: *Encarta and MSN*

CHAPTER 5

THE JUDICIARY

The less popular, but very important, third branch of government is the **Judiciary,** or the courts. As outlined in the Constitution, the role of the judiciary is to interpret the law. The Supreme Court was established by the Constitution as the highest court in the country. Most federal cases, however, are heard in lower courts that have been established by Congress. Most federal judges are nominated by the president, after which they must be confirmed by the Senate. Federal judges serve for as long as they wish, either until death or retirement. The only way to force out a federal judge is to impeach him.

The federal court system deals with federal crimes and federal law in both criminal and civil cases. The legal system in this country provides for state laws and courts, as well as federal laws and courts. The federal court system deals with laws that affect the entire nation and deals with serious crimes that fall under the jurisdiction of those laws.

District Courts

Congress has established 94 **District Courts** throughout the country in certain geographical areas. The district court is where criminal cases involving violations of federal law are tried, such as money counterfeiting, bank robbery, and mail fraud. The district court's original jurisdiction allows civil cases that involve rights, not crimes, or questions of the constitutionality of a law to be heard.

The district court also has appellate jurisdiction, meaning that cases that have gone through the state system without being resolved may be appealed to the federal district court.

In criminal cases that appear before the district courts, the **U.S. Attorney's Office** is the prosecuting arm of the government. This office falls under the command of the Justice Department. Each federal district has such an office with a U.S. Attorney who is appointed by the president with the traditional approval of the senators of the state from the president's party where the district court operates. Like most other appointments, the selection of U.S. Attorneys is very political, and those who are selected are almost always from the president's party. The appointment of judges and lawyers who are from the same party gives the president the ability to implement his ideology through those who think like him and to keep the country moving forward. There are no prosecutors in civil cases. In a civil case, you have a plaintiff, who makes the charge of wrongdoing or illegality against the defendant.

The **U.S. Marshals** are the ones who transport federal prisoners, and who hunt down fugitives, or people who have run away from the law after committing a crime. U.S. Marshals travel around the world to bring Americans home to justice.

U.S. Court of Appeals

Decisions made by a district court, as well as by federal agencies, can be appealed to one of the nation's 13 circuits (districts) of the **U.S. Court of Appeals.** Three judges sit on each appellate court, and decisions are based on a majority vote. Nearly 50,000 cases are brought up every year through the appellate courts where they are usually resolved.

The Supreme Court

The **Supreme Court** is currently comprised of nine **Justices**, but that number is not a permanent one. The leader of the Court is known as the **Chief Justice**. This body is the final stop in the appeals process. The chances of getting a case heard by the Supreme Court are very small. Some 7,000 requests are made every year for cases to be decided by the Court, but only around 100 are selected. Requests are made by lawyers who wish to appeal their clients' cases to the Supreme Court by filing a *writ of certiorari*, which asks that the issues involved in the case be addressed by the Court.

The Court usually hears cases that pose new challenges to the enforcement of law, as well as to certain laws themselves. The court's decision on whether a law is legal according to the Constitution is called **Judicial Review.** For example, the legality of certain sections of the USA PATRIOT Act, which are viewed by some as violating civil liberties, is an issue that can be appealed to the Supreme Court. The power given to law enforcement by those sections can be struck down as unconstitutional, whereby the government will be forbidden from using them, unless of course the Constitution is amended. There is no guarantee that the Court will hear a case in the first place, let alone rule that a law that is challenged is unconstitutional.

A simple majority of 5 out of 9 is needed to approve a decision. Once decisions among the justices are made, an opinion will be issued stating the reasons for the decision. If the vote was not unanimous, justices opposing the decision will usually issue a dissenting opinion offering their perspective on the case.

The nomination of judges is probably one of the most politically and ideologically charged actions that a president takes. The make-up of the Court reflects the ideological differences that various presidents over the years have had. Some justices are conservative, some liberal. There are two female justices, one of whom happens to be Jewish, one black justice, and one Catholic justice, all of whom sit on the Court, not just because of their qualifications, but because of the political statement that having women and persons of particular religious and ethnic backgrounds make about the political mood of the society. Often, justices will hold off retiring from their posts until a president who shares the same ideology as them is elected to make sure that the new judge will maintain the representation of that ideology in the Court.

DID YOU KNOW?

U.S. District Judge Alcee Hastings of Florida was charged with perjury and conspiring to obtain a bribe, and was impeached, convicted, and removed from office on October 20, 1989. In 1992, he was elected to serve in Congress and is currently a member of the Democratic leadership in the House of Representatives, the same body that impeached him.

Although he was impeached and convicted, the Senate did not ban him from seeking public office in the future, a punishment that it could have imposed on him if it desired to do so.

CHAPTER 6

STATE AND LOCAL GOVERNMENTS

As much as our lives are affected by decisions made in Washington, they are perhaps more affected by what happens in our own states, counties, and cities. The layers of government may sometimes be confusing and jurisdictions are often blurred. There are so many layers because the Constitution gives the people all rights that are not delegated to the government. States have their own constitutions and laws, but these cannot be in violation of the U.S. Constitution and federal law.

Jurisdiction

There is the state government, whose officials are elected by all citizens of the state and whose purpose is to serve everyone in the state. Then you have the county government, responsible for the things that the state government does not do and only for the people within the county. Inside the county you may have a city, which has its own government, and there are also townships with many villages within the county. All have their own local governments to perform certain responsibilities.

An example is Illinois, with 102 counties and hundreds of other local jurisdictions--either cities, towns or villages. Each jurisdiction has its own police force to keep the peace and enforce the law.

The city of Burbank, IL, for instance, like all other jurisdictions must enforce all state laws. Burbank is one of several cities in Cook County, so the laws of the county must be enforced as well. In addition to those laws, the Burbank police must enforce the laws made by Stickney Township, which it is part of, as well as local laws, or ordinances as they are called, made by the Burbank City Council. If it is illegal for a vehicle to have a "For Sale" sign in its window in neighboring Oak Lawn but not in Burbank, then the Burbank police do not have the responsibility nor the right to enforce that law on vehicles within its city limits. However, if state law prohibits the use of tinted windows on vehicles, then the Burbank police must enforce that law.

Executive Branch

Just like the federal government, state and local governments follow the separation of powers model of a three-branch government. At the state level, the one who runs the government is the **Governor**. This person is elected by the people of the state. To assist him, the people may elect a **Lieutenant Governor**, just like the president and vice president. Each state has its own rules and structure. Some states may require the election of state officials like the **Attorney General** or the **Treasurer**. In other states, those officials may be appointed by the governor. It's the job of the governor and his staff to come up with a state budget every year and to implement and oversee programs statewide. Education, healthcare, and unemployment are some of the top priorities of state government, as are crime and transportation. The state government, like the federal government, gets money for its programs and functioning by raising taxes. In addition to tax revenues, states get grants (money) from the federal government for certain projects like the building of roads and bridges and to administer programs like Medicare and welfare.

Counties are usually run by a board of commissioners or trustees with the leader being the **Board President, Chairman**, or **County Executive**. The role of the county government depends on the size and makeup of the county. Baltimore County in Maryland, for instance, is dominated by the city of Baltimore, so there are a lot of gray areas of jurisdiction and power. South of Baltimore County is Ann Arundel County, which has no major cities within its boundaries, and whose residents rely heavily on its emergency services, libraries, and community college. The board in Ann Arundel County has more governmental power because it does not have to compete with a large city within its borders.

At the city, or municipal, level, a **Mayor** is elected to run the government. Usually the mayor appoints the heads of the city's various departments, i.e. police, fire, health, public works, parks, and so forth. Keeping the streets of the city clean and safe are major responsibilities for city mayors. They also must work hard to keep their local economies in good shape. When companies and stores are open, people are working, they're spending money, and the municipality (city) is collecting taxes to run its operations.

The township and village governments are microcosms (small examples) of the county and city government relationships and roles. A county may have within its borders two or three small cities, and three or four townships. Each township may have anywhere from one to five villages under its jurisdiction. The township has its board of trustees or supervisors, and the villages have their city councils.

All of these layers of government may seem needless and wasteful. Perhaps this may be true, but for a long time, they have been at the heart of the political makeup of this country, especially in states with more urban areas. This system has been used as a roadmap for groups, political or otherwise, to gain power in this country. Before they run their members for Congress, they make sure that they have members on the city councils and school boards. This is why former House Speaker Tip O'Neill said "all politics is local"--because there are levels of government that one has to master and control before there can be success at the next level.

Legislative Branch

This branch of state and local government that makes the laws is very closely connected to the executive branch because as the jurisdiction gets more local in nature, government gets smaller. Villages and cities have councils, whose members represent people who live in wards. These councils create ordinances that only apply to their residents. The greatest, and often controversial, issue that is dealt with at this level is property tax. Every person who owns a home, building, or piece of land must pay property tax. This tax is used mainly to pay for the public school system. If the school system is in need of more money, the council may try to raise property taxes. This may not be a popular thing with the residents of the city or village. Often, a referendum, or a vote by the people, will take place on Election Day. People will have the chance to vote for or against a tax increase, and the outcome of that vote will be the ultimate decision.

Other issues that these local councils deal with are zoning laws. City planners designate pieces of land as commercial or residential. If the corner of a street is zoned only for commercial use, then only a business can be established there. If it is zoned for residential use only, then a house or apartment building will be the only proper structure to be built there. These laws change from time to time, and residents can lobby the council to change the status of a piece of land. This is known as a variance.

One way that councilmen have tried to block the building of mosques in their areas is by refusing to change the zoning status of the land where a mosque is to be built or expanded. In other positive instances, zoning laws have been changed specifically for new mosques to be established.

At the county and township level, the board of commissioners or trustees are responsible for making the rules. Sometimes the board also serves as an executive branch, while other times a board president, chairman, or executive is elected by the people.

The state legislature is probably the one that is most independent from the executive branch of government. Most state legislatures or assemblies are bicameral, with a House and a Senate. Nebraska is the only state to be unicameral with only one legislative chamber. The California State Assembly has 40 senators and 80 representatives. As in the U.S. Congress, the areas represented by state senators are larger than representative districts. In fact state assemblies have a lot in common with Congress. There are House speakers and Senate presidents. The legislative process involves bills that go to committees before being voted on in the full chamber. Actually a great many members of the U.S.

Congress had served at one time or another in their state assemblies, so it is also a great political stepping stone for those who wish to have successful political careers.

Table 5: Some Responsibilities and Powers of Government

Federal	Make laws for the entire nation. Enforcing federal law. Provide national defense. Produce money. Protect citizens from fraud. Raise taxes for programs and operations.
State	Overseeing property rights. Maintaining roads. Education of citizens. Making laws for the entire state. Enforcing state and federal laws. Raise taxes for programs and operations.
County	Law enforcement. Maintaining records and vital statistics. Building and maintaining local roads. Running local medical facilities. Providing assistance to the poor. Making laws for the entire county. Enforcing county, state and federal laws. Raise taxes for programs and operations.
City	Make laws for the entire city. Enforce city, county, state and federal laws. Trash collection. Maintain public schools. Zoning of property. Issue building permits and business licenses. Raise taxes for programs and operations.
Township	Responsible for water supply and wastewater management. Enforces zoning and building codes. Provide services on behalf of the county or state.
School Board	Approves curriculum to be taught. Oversight of school administration and faculty.

Note: Responsibilities and powers vary at the county, city, and township level.

Figure 2: *Relationship Between Local, State and Federal Government*

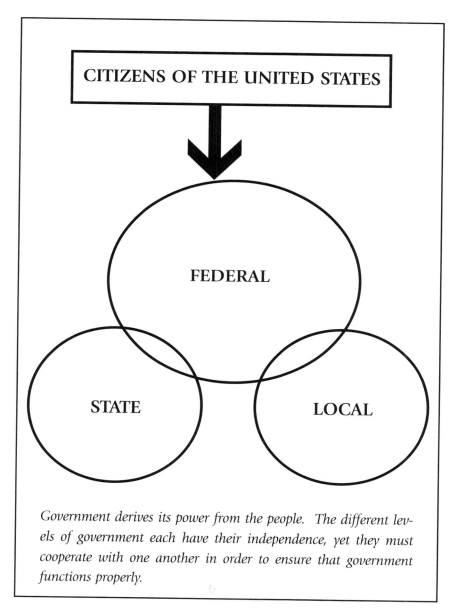

Government derives its power from the people. The different levels of government each have their independence, yet they must cooperate with one another in order to ensure that government functions properly.

Judicial Branch

Most municipalities have their own courts or hearings for traffic-related violations or violations of local ordinances. The bulk of court cases is heard before county superior, or circuit courts. There may be one or more of such courts within a county depending on its size and population. Both criminal and civil cases appear before the judges of these courts. Most judges in the state court system are elected by the people, not appointed, like federal judges. The criminal cases they hear involve violent and non-violent crimes committed against a person or society at large. The **District Attorney's Office (DA)** is responsible for representing the people of the state in seeking justice in such cases. **Assistant District Attorneys** prosecute those charged with a crime in open court. The accused is innocent until the DA can prove without a doubt that he is guilty. The evidence may be very clear and the accused may plead guilty, or he may maintain a plea of innocence and request to be tried before a jury of 12 citizens. If a defendant cannot afford an attorney, the judge will appoint a **Public Defender** to represent him in court. An accused person does have the right to represent himself, but those who study and practice law agree that doing so is about the most foolish thing that one can do while being tried for a crime.

Civil cases, as discussed previously in Chapter 5, involve issues related to property, business deals, divorces, and individual rights. The one who is making the accusation is the plaintiff, and the one who is the accused is the defendant. If many people believe they have been wronged by a company or government body, they may file what is known as a class-action lawsuit to avoid separate trials, and to show a clear pattern of wrongdoing by the defendant.

If a person loses a trial, he may appeal the verdict based on legal reasons. That case will then be heard before an Appellate Court, which will either uphold the original verdict, reverse the lower court's verdict, or throw out the verdict altogether and call for a new trial. A panel of judges, not a jury, decides the case by a simple majority vote.

The last resort for an appeal in the state court system is the State Supreme Court. If a defendant appeals the verdict of the Appellate Court to the state Supreme Court, they will ask for a final verdict by the state. State Supreme Court justices come to decisions by majority vote, and their verdict is final as far as the state is concerned. If a person wishes to take a case further, his only option is the federal court system. Cases that start at the circuit court level and end up at the U.S. Supreme Court may take years of moving up the court ladder, and in the case of civil lawsuits, may cost millions of dollars.

DID YOU KNOW?

Below is a list of some local laws that actually have been passed over the years.

Alaska--No child is to build a snowman taller than himself on school property.

Arkansas--A man may beat his wife, but no more than once a month.

California--Women are prohibited from driving their vehicles while dressed in a robe.

Indiana--It is illegal to make a monkey smoke a cigarette.

New Jersey--It is illegal to wear a bulletproof vest while committing a murder.

Source: *Various state statutes.*

CHAPTER 7

POLITICAL PARTIES

A major pillar in the foundation of American politics is the political party. Unlike other nations, the United States has a **two-party system** that allows for two major parties to run the government, although the parties themselves are not part of the government. The **Democratic Party** and the **Republican Party** unite Americans who hold similar ideologies to work together to control bodies of government at the local, state, and national level. The main job of the two parties is to run candidates for office during election time. It is the nature of these and other political parties to get large numbers of people to support the party by volunteering for campaigns, donating money, and voting for the party's candidates. In return, those elected officials pay back their party and supporters by working for policies and programs that will please the party "faithful" and benefit those who helped get them into office.

Although the two-party system is the basis for political activity in this country, other **third parties** have the full right to organize and run candidates for office just as the Democrats and Republicans do. Because of the winner-take-all nature of elections (the one with the most votes wins), third parties rarely have the opportunity to gather the votes necessary to win an election.

Structure

Membership into the Republican and Democratic parties is pretty simple--all you have to do is vote for their candidates at election time or declare your party membership when you register to vote. So tens of millions of Americans are members of either of the two main political parties, many of whom do not even realize it. The parties themselves are run by active members and elected officials at the local, state, and national level. Locally, parties are usually organized by committees at the county level, with **Committeemen** usually being those party members who are most effective at raising money or generating votes on Election Day. These county committees focus on running members of their party for elected office. At the state level, the parties pool all of their power and resources to run candidates for statewide office. The **State Party Chairmen** are among the most powerful people in the American political community. Nationally, each party has a committee to organize the party conventions that happen every four years, support state and local committees in their election efforts, and run the overall party operations.

Headquartered in Washington, DC, the **Republican National Committee (RNC)** manages the party and assists elected officials in promoting the agenda of the party. At the national convention every four years, delegations from each of the 50 states nominate one national committeeman and one national committeewoman to represent them in the RNC. The chairman of their state's party is automatically appointed to the RNC. The party's candidate for president elects the chairman of the RNC, who heads the 11-member executive committee, which has administrative and some policy responsibilities. The RNC has several internal committees to deal with things like arrangements for the national convention and fundraising. Members of the Republican Party are mostly Caucasian, but the party has been reaching out to emerging political powers like Hispanic-Americans, estimated to be one-fourth of the nation's population by 2025. There is a strong emphasis on drawing women into the party, as evident by the gender quotas in the makeup of the national committee. Republicans are generally considered to be conservative, but within the party there is a right-wing faction, or group, headed by Christian fundamentalists like Franklin Graham and Jerry Falwell, who are pretty much anti-Muslim and anti-minorities. This faction is very pro-Israel as well. Then there are moderate Republicans who want to change the party and make it more inclusive. These factions often disagree on ideological issues, but for the most part are very well disciplined and united.

The structure of the **Democratic National Committee (DNC)** is slightly different than the RNC. Although the general membership of the party is the same (i.e. those who vote for Democrats), the DNC has a governing body of 400 party leaders, activists, and elected officials. The DNC is not as centralized as the RNC, and it works to coordinate efforts with state and local party chapters. The DNC prepares for its national convention virtually in the same manner as the RNC. Democrats are mostly middle and working-class Americans from various ethnic backgrounds. There are many more factions within the Democratic Party, and thus unity has sometimes been a problem. All the way on the left of the political spectrum within the party you have feminist and gay rights groups. On the other side you have conservative Democrats who share some of the views of Republicans, but remain loyal Democrats. President Bill Clinton was a conservative Democrat, while Congressman Barney Frank (D-MA), who is openly gay, is what Republicans love to call a "left-wing liberal."

Ideology

Fundamental positions on issues are what usually define the ideologies of the two parties, although members do not always agree 100% with the party platform, or the agenda that is set and agreed upon at the national convention every four years.

Democrats are usually pro-choice when it comes to abortion, they are against the death penalty, they believe it is the government's job to provide social services for the needy, they favor the rights of workers and labor unions over those of corporations, and they work to preserve the environment from pollution. Gun control and civil rights are also important issues for Democrats.

Republicans are generally pro-life, pro-death penalty, pro-gun rights, and pro-business. Big government is an enemy to Republicans. To them, government has too much power as it is, and it is too wasteful. Traditional family values and a strong approach to crime-fighting are championed by Republicans.

With regard to the economy, Democrats support higher taxes for the rich and tax breaks for working-class Americans. Republicans fight for tax breaks for the rich and government assistance to large struggling corporations. After 9/11, billions of dollars were given to corporations to help them survive and to give a boost to the weak economy. Democrats call this "corporate welfare."

There is not much of a difference between the two parties when it comes to foreign policy. Their views of the world, however, and how to interact with other nations are founded in their realistic and idealistic perspectives. Republicans are generally **realists**, believing that the power of the state (also means country) is the most important thing in a world of people who are fundamentally evil and selfish in their intentions. Democrats are usually **idealists**, believing that humans are generally good and that diplomacy must always be the answer to conflict. Force should be the last resort in solving international disputes. This divide was very noticeable as the United States invaded Iraq in 2003, with the nation split between Republicans who supported President Bush's policy of preemption and regime change, and by Democrats who felt that war on Iraq was unjustified since Iraq had not attacked America. Democrats were also concerned about the damage that was being caused to America's reputation in the world by such unilateral actions.

Both ideologies are changing however, as the world changes through social development and globalization. Muslim-Americans have been struggling to choose between the two parties for a long time. The Democratic Party, which is inclusive and active on civil rights issues, seems like a good choice for Muslims. However, the pro-choice stance on abortion and the affiliation with gay and lesbian groups makes Muslims feel uncomfortable because of their religious beliefs and values.

The Republican Party with its anti-abortion position and its emphasis on family values perhaps is ideal for Muslims, especially for those who are small-business owners. The problem with this party, however, is that, traditionally, it has not been as inclusive as the Democrats. Furthermore, there has been much anti-Muslim rhetoric coming from Republicans, like New York Congressman Peter Kink, who said that 85% of American mosques are run by extremists and that they are "an enemy amongst us," or Christian televangelist Pat Robertson, who has made numerous hate-filled comments regarding Islam, calling it an "evil religion," and claiming that Muslims are "worse than the Nazis."

Individually, many Muslims have made the choice to join one party or the other. At the national level, however, Muslim-American organizations have supported candidates from both parties, without throwing their support behind a specific party.

Which party will Muslims choose to be a part of as a community? The answer is really up to the parties themselves. The party that is most interested in the support and membership of the Muslim community will be sure to win it over. Perhaps Muslims will never join a party as a national community and continue to vote for candidates based on their own merits, and not their party affiliation. Only time will tell.

As individuals, picking a political party to join, if any, depends a lot upon the local party, which may be more appealing or unattractive than the national party. A wise approach to joining a party is determining which party will address your issues more, and which party will be more welcoming to you and people like you.

Third Parties

Smaller, third parties have long been part of the American political process, which discourages the creation of more than two political parties. Those who push for third parties usually break away from one of the two mainstream parties because of differences on policy and ideology. Other Americans have formed third parties because the Democratic and Republican parties are seen as two different wings of the same party. For whatever reason they are formed, third parties represent a desire for change in America. Some are taken seriously by the political establishment, while others are ignored altogether. When third parties run candidates for election, they give voters the opportunity to cast "protest votes" to signal their dissatisfaction with the two major parties.

Third parties have been very limited in their effectiveness at the voting polls. Some parties have won seats in local and state elections, but winning federal office has thus far been impossible, mainly because of the limited popularity of their ideologies and because of their lack of proper financial resources to launch effective campaigns. A major test of a third party is if it can get at least 5% of the popular vote during a presidential election. If it does that, it will be recognized by the government as a national political organization and it will get some funding for its campaigns. Over the past decade, there have been three minor political parties that have gained people's attention: the **Libertarian Party**, the **Reform Party**, and the **Green Party**.

The Libertarian Party claims that it is the largest third party in the nation. The ideology that drives this party is of a right-wing nature. The Libertarian website reads, "Each individual has the right to control his or her own body, action, speech, and property. Government's only role is to help individuals defend themselves from force and fraud."

Libertarians don't want government to interfere so much in the lives of citizens. They claim that people should be able to do whatever they want, and that there should be no control on business. This train of thought is similar to **Social Darwinism**, or the belief that humans are constantly engaged in conflict as society develops. What determines who will win these contests is the notion of the "survival of the fittest," meaning those who are more able will survive and those who are not able will die.

In 1992, millionaire Ross Perot went on CNN's "Larry King Live" and talked about how disconnected the political parties were with the people and how corrupt and inefficient the government had become. He offered to run for president if the people asked him to. Over the next few months, 5 million people took him up on his offer by signing petitions in all 50 states of the union to get Perot's name on the ballot for the presidential elections. Perot had triggered a mini revolution in America by giving people who were frustrated with the political process a chance to have their voices heard. In November of that year, over 19 million people voted for Perot. This accomplishment was a major achievement for the thousands of volunteers who worked for reforming the government.

Over the next few years, **United We Stand America (UWSA)**, the umbrella organization established by Perot, served as a government "watchdog" group, looking out for corruption and inefficiencies in government. Perot ran again in 1996, but only got about 9% of the vote as opposed to the 20% he got in 1992. Shortly after the 1996 elections, the members of UWSA established the **Reform Party U.S.A**. This new national party's platform barely represented the sentiments of the early reformers of 1992. Among the founding principals of the Reform Party are for elections to be held on the weekend instead of Tuesdays, to eliminate the Electoral College (discussed in next chapter), to withdraw the United States from NATO, the United Nations, and all other treaties, to recognize America's historical Christian roots, and to eliminate laws that classify crimes as "hate crimes." Many UWSA members had objected to the hijacking of the party by right-wing elements, and so they left the Reform Party U.S.A. and established the **American Reform Party.** There was yet another split in the Reform Party during the 2000 elections when factions within the party fought for control of the leadership and control of some $5 million that the party would get from the federal government to assist in their candidate's campaign for president. For those who were inspired by Ross Perot and dreamed of changing their country for the better, frustration has again taken over.

Although it is very active and well-known in Europe, the **Green Party** has not been as popular in this country, that is, not until the 2000 presidential elections. The American branch of the Green Party is a confederation of state parties. The fundamentals of the party's ideology are: protection of the environment, non-violence, social justice, and grassroots democracy. According to its mission, "Greens are renewing citizen democracy without the support of corporate donors."

In the 2000 elections, Ralph Nader, the most famous advocate of consumer rights in America, ran for president on the Green Party's ticket. Nader attracted many to his campaign, especially Perot-era reformers and liberal Democrats. Mainstream Democrats, however, criticized Nader and the Greens because they felt that those who gave their vote to

Nader would take away a vote from the Democrats and, in effect, help their common enemy, the Republicans. The Greens resisted this argument saying that their issues are more important than politics and that the Democratic leadership has not been serious enough about the issues that are important to them.

Nader, himself an Arab-American, spoke of a fair foreign policy with justice and freedom for all peoples of the world, including the Palestinians. In fact many Muslims volunteered for Nader's campaign and pressure was put on the political leadership of the Muslim community to endorse Nader for president. It was guaranteed, however, that Nader would lose the election. The Muslim community's rationale behind not endorsing Nader was that they would have achieved little by backing him outside of the Muslims using their vote as a form of protest.

Nader threw his hat into the presidential ring again in 2004, but this time as an independent candidate. The Green Party, which nominated him in 2000, declined to do so a second time.

The debate in the Muslim community of whether or not to back third party or independent candidates out of moral conviction will continue for a long time to come. There are legitimate views on both sides of the argument.

If Muslims back a third party candidate for president and make sure that the Democrats and Republicans know that they are doing so because they are not satisfied with either party, then perhaps after the election, the major parties will pay more attention to Muslim-American voters, especially if they can prove that their votes number over one million.

Alternatively, there is another view that Muslims are already on the margins of politics, and so if they join others who are on the margins, they will create a coalition of the marginalized and remain isolated from the power structures of the country. One may argue that the pie of political power is limited, and that it is divided between two parties. If a third party attempts to take a share of the pie, it will find resistance from both parties, as neither wants to give up any of its share of the pie.

DID YOU KNOW?

Although Ralph Nader was nominated as the Green Party's presidential candidate in 2000, he wasn't actually a member of the Green Party.

CHAPTER 8

THE VOTING PROCESS

Since America has a "republican" form of government (government of the people, by the people, and for the people), it is the responsibility of citizens to cast their votes for those who represent them at every level of government. Many Americans take this responsibility very seriously, especially war veterans who fought for the ideals and values of this nation. It is common for Americans, especially many proud immigrants who fled persecution in their home countries, to get dressed in their best clothes and take their children with them to the voting polls as they exercise their right, and fulfill their responsibility of citizenship. Many Americans take a cynical view of politics and refuse to vote because they feel that their vote will not make a change. Other Americans simply do not know about the importance of voting and the electoral process, or they simply just do not care.

Any citizen of the United States, whether born here or elsewhere, has the right to vote in elections. Green card holders and other non-citizen residents do not have the right to vote in governmental elections. As discussed in previous chapters, not every American had the right to vote. Before 1870, blacks could not vote. Before 1920, women did not have the right to vote. And before 1971, citizens who were under 21 in every state except Georgia, even those over the age of 18 who served in the military, did not have the right to vote. In each case it took a constitutional amendment in order to allow for new voting rights for each group.

Immigrants who can't legally vote still have a major role to play in the political empowerment of the Muslim community, and thus, they should not feel as if they can't make a difference simply because they are ineligible to vote.

Candidates and Voting

A candidate is someone who is seeking election to a government office. To increase the chances of winning, a candidate will seek to represent a political party in the elections. More than one candidate may seek the endorsement or nomination of his or her political party, but only one person can actually run as that party's candidate in the official, or **general election**, usually held in November. Therefore political parties select one person out of a larger group by having a **primary election**, where party members vote for the person they want to represent them in the general election. Alternatively, a state party may have a convention or caucus where delegates choose who will represent the party. Sometimes, cities or states will have **run-off** elections for the two candidates with the most votes in an election with many candidates, none of whom won a majority of the vote (i.e. more than 50%). **Special elections** are held at a time other than the scheduled election date for offices whose occupants have died, resigned, or have been recalled.

The people have the power to remove an elected official from office by having what is known as a **Recall**. In 2003, the citizens of California were so upset with the performance of Democratic Governor Gray Davis that they recalled, or fired, him from office and replaced him with Republican Arnold Schwarzenegger, a Hollywood actor who was born in Austria and who had never been elected to public office before winning the governorship.

In local politics, parties do not usually have primaries. The Democratic Party in St. Louis, for instance may run many individuals for different local offices on a **Slate**, or a list of candidates chosen by the party. The slate is presented to voters who are asked to vote for everyone on the slate. Big names on the slate assist others who are not so well known. The overall goal is to get everyone from the Democratic Party elected together. Candidates can run as independents, but their chances of success are much lower than party candidates because they will not have the resources of the party to back them up during the election. It takes an awfully popular person to win an election as an independent. Many Muslims have won elections for public office in local and state elections as candidates for both parties *(See Profile of Muslims in Government in Appendix II)*.

In order to vote for candidates, citizens must register to vote, usually no later than 30 days before Election Day. Once citizens register the first time, they do not need to do it again unless they move. After registering, citizens receive voter identification cards with their name, address, precinct number, and polling station. The precinct is the local voting area where citizens live, and the polling station is where votes are actually cast, or made. Usually, polling stations are used by many neighborhood precincts, and they are open from the early hours of the morning until the evening. Fire stations, schools, community centers, and even churches are typical polling stations. In Bridgeview, Illinois, Muslims have suc-ceeded in having the Universal School, a private Islamic insti-tution, designated as a polling place.

Many states have **Motor Voter** laws that allow people to register to vote when they get their driver's licenses. Traditionally, citizens are registered to vote by volunteers in their communities or by contacting their local board of elec-tions and filing the proper form. Political parties and inter-est groups try to recruit new supporters by sending out voter registration volunteers to malls, colleges, and even door-to-door to register those who are not already registered. This is important to the party or group because they keep a copy of the registration application and put it in their files of people they know are registered to vote. During election season, they will send those whom they registered political literature urg-ing them to vote for the candidates of their choice. Today, people can register to vote on the Internet through their county government, political parties, or interest groups. They simply fill out the voter registration form on their computer, print it, sign it, and send it in the mail. Actual online voter registration is still not allowed. It may be sometime before Congress passes a law allowing citizens to complete the entire voter registration process on the Internet.

When a person goes to vote, they must take their voter identification card with them. They will present this card to an election judge sitting at the voter's precinct table. The voter is then given a ballot with either the names of the can-didates or numbers that the voter will punch with a small tool. Voting methods vary from county to county. Voters then enter private booths where they make their choices for various public offices.

After the 2000 elections, electronic voting machines began replacing the old punch card system in order to make voting simpler and vote counting more accurate. These computerized machines were put to the test in the 2002 election cycle. The results were mixed. There were several reports of technical problems that delayed or prevented people from voting.

In 2001, a group of experts from the Information Security Institute (ISI) at Johns Hopkins University concluded that electronic voting machines were vulnerable to hackers who could easily break into the machine's hard drive and alter the outcome of an election without leaving a trace.

In a **presidential election year**, the voter will select candidates for the presidency, for Congress, maybe for the Senate, for state offices, for local offices, and judges. Voters may also perhaps vote on a referendum that may deal with property taxes or other local issues. In a **midterm election**, which is two years after each presidential election year, there may be no candidates running for major offices other than congressmen. The ballot of candidates may only have the names of people running for a few local or state races.

Research has proved that the higher the education level of a person and the more money that he/she has, the greater the likelihood of him/her voting.

Voter Turnout, or the number of registered voters who actually vote on Election Day, is much higher during presidential election years than during midterm elections. So the number of people actually voting in an election may only be 30% of the eligible voters, and only 10% of the entire population. This is important because if Muslims make up, let's say, 5% of eligible voters in a state, then they can multiply their impact on an election if 100% of eligible Muslims vote on Election Day, and vote for the same candidate. If only 25% of eligible voters went to the polls on that day, the Muslims' 5% would be multiplied by four to 20%. And if they all voted for the same candidates, they would for sure be the deciding factor in the election of a candidate. This is known as **block voting.**

Many citizens may not be able to vote in person because they are away serving in the military, or going to college in another state. Voters can request to cast their votes through an **absentee ballot**, which is sent to them by mail, filled out, and then sent back to the local elections commission in their home county where they are registered.

Campaigns

To win over the hearts and votes of constituents, candidates run campaigns to get themselves elected. There are two types of candidates, **incumbents** and **challengers**. The incumbent is the one who already holds the office and is seeking re-election. The challenger is the one who tries to defeat the incumbent and take over his or her position. Some races are **open-seat races**, where there is no incumbent seeking re-election. Those running for an open seat are simply called candidates.

The goal of the campaign is to get the candidate's name and message out to the public. Name recognition is important in a campaign because when a person is in the voting booth making a decision, he/she may only vote for candidates whose names he/she remembers. Some candidates do not have a problem with name recognition. In 1998, the Reform Party's candidate for governor in Minnesota was Jesse "The Body" Ventura, a former professional wrestler turned

86

politician. Since he was a celebrity, people knew his name and were interested in hearing his position on the issues. Ventura won the election beating candidates from the two major parties. Former First Lady Hillary Clinton moved to New York State towards the end of her husband's final term as president so that she should could establish her residency early enough to run for the Senate. Clinton, having lived in New York for less than two years, won the Senate race in 2000, with the popularity of her name carrying her the entire way.

There are other key factors to the success of a campaign, the main one these days being money. It is very common for candidates in congressional and Senate races to spend millions of dollars on TV and radio ads, billboards, and mailings to the homes of constituents. This need for strong financial resources gives those who are rich an advantage over those who do not have the personal wealth to spend on campaigns. Still, candidates rely heavily on contributions from constituents, party supporters, and political action committees, known as PACs. Candidates running for important offices may get a lot of fundraising help from the state party, or even the party's national committee. Billionaire Michael Bloomberg, a man who has never held any public office, spent $76 million of his own money when he ran as a Republican for the mayor's office in New York City in 2001. He won, replacing outgoing mayor Rudolph Guiliani.

The **Federal Election Commission (FEC)** limits the amount of money that people can contribute to a congressional, senatorial, or presidential campaign to $2,000 per person, or $4,000 from a couple with a joint bank account. These limits apply to each separate election. The FEC rules indicate that primary, run-off, and general elections are separate from one another, so one can legally contribute the maximum amount to their favored candidate if, for instance, they must run in a primary election in March and then a general election in November. Under this scenario, an individual could contribute a total of $4,000 and a couple could give $8,000.

PACs can give up to $5,000 per candidate. Individuals can also give money to political parties, up to $25,000 per year. The total combined amount that a person contributes to political campaigns cannot be over $95,000 every two years. Only American citizens and resident aliens who hold Green Cards are allowed to contribute to political campaigns. Business owners who have a contract with the government cannot contribute money to federal campaigns, so that they are not seen as buying influence. Tax-exempt non-profit organizations like mosques, schools, and charities cannot contribute funds to political campaigns. Mosques can allow candidates to address their congregations and they can have committees to discuss political issues, but they cannot officially support one party or candidate over another.

Those who contribute a lot of money to a campaign expect something in return, i.e. support for one issue or another. This may be a gamble on the part of the contributor because his/her contribution does not guarantee that the candidate will support his/her policy. This lesson has not been learned by many Muslims who are excited about meeting politicians and give them money without getting any guarantees from the politician on how he/she will vote on issues of importance to Muslims. Thousands of Muslim political dollars are wasted every year on politicians who sit down, listen to what Muslims have to say, and quietly take their money, knowing that they will not support the Muslim's cause. Politicians should be approached like businessmen, and not dignitaries. Money and votes are the most important things to them, and if you can offer either of those things, then you should ask for something in return. If you have enough money or votes, you probably will in fact get something in return. This is known as *quid pro quo*, which literally means "something for something."

Many political activists in the Muslim community have grown increasingly frustrated with the "ceremonial" approach to politics that is often taken. These activists warn that being satisfied with taking pictures with politicians or with inviting them to the mosque for falafel and hummus cannot be the Muslim approach to politics. They encourage serious engagement with politicians on issues that are clearly important to the community that they claim to represent. Furthermore, politicians are very keen at recognizing the level of political maturity and seriousness that a group has when he/she meets with them. If a group comes off as being happy just to be in the same room with this politician, he/she will take advantage of that and keep the ceremony going in order to avoid discussing real policy issues. Far too many Muslims have been meeting with politicians and donating thousands to their campaigns only to be left with a slap on the back and a wall full of pictures.

Another key factor in the success of a campaign is volunteers. Having volunteers to assist in passing out campaign literature, making phone calls, and collecting contributions is one of the most valuable assets to a campaign, especially one that is run on a tight budget. In return for their service, volunteers get political experience that may help them one day to run their own campaign. College students may even get credit for their activities on a campaign. Those who volunteer for a campaign because of a candidate's position on an important issue get the satisfaction of knowing they are helping to try to get someone who will fight for their cause if elected. Campaigns give Muslims a great opportunity to make *da'wah* by introducing themselves as Muslim-Americans to non-Muslims. This defeats ignorance, and it will contribute to the acceptance of Muslims by the rest of America.

Endorsements

Since a candidate's goal is to get as many people to vote for him as possible, he will seek the **endorsement**, or approval and support, of community groups, labor unions, and associations, whose memberships tend to vote for the candidates that have been endorsed by their organization. Candidates may also get endorsements from newspapers, usually in the days or weeks prior to the election. Among the most important endorsements that candidates receive are those from the **American Association of Retired Persons (AARP)**, the largest senior citizens group in the country with chapters in every state, and the **American Federation of Labor and Congress of Industrial Organizations (AFL-CIO)**, the largest federation of labor unions in the country.

Endorsements are based on many factors. Groups decide on who will better serve their interests while in office. They may demand something from a candidate in return for an endorsement, or the candidate may offer something before it is even asked of him to show how badly the endorsement of that particular group is desired.

The American-Muslim Political Coordinating Council (AMPCC) was the coalition of national Islamic organizations that endorsed George W. Bush for president in 2000. The main four members of AMPCC were the **American Muslim Alliance (AMA)**, the **American Muslim Council (AMC)**, the **Council on American-Islamic Relations (CAIR)**, and the **Muslim Public Affairs Council (MPAC)**.

Dr. Agha Saeed, chairman of the AMA, was the founding chairman of AMPCC, which in 2004 was changed to the American Muslim Task Force for Elections and Civil Rights. He led the effort to evaluate all of the candidates for president based on domestic policy issues and on how the candidates dealt with Muslim-Americans. According to Saeed, Democrat Al Gore never responded to requests for a meeting by AMPCC. On the contrary, the Bush campaign first reached out to the Muslims. What made AMPCC's endorsement of Bush final was when Bush, during the second of three nationally televised debates with Al Gore, condemned the use of secret evidence. Saeed has rejected the argument that Muslims made a mistake by supporting Bush for president. "We did not base our decision on foreign policy because we knew both candidates weren't much different from each other in that aspect," said Saeed at the 5th annual convention of the **Islamic Association for Palestine (IAP)**, held in Chicago in December 2001.

Many agree with Saeed arguing that Muslim voting power will not be realized in one election, and that the 2000 elections were part of the development of the community's political activism. Former Congressman Paul Findley has taken it further than that. In a *January/February 2001* article in the ***Washington Report on Middle East Affairs*** magazine, Findley argued that over 60,000 Muslims had voted for Bush in Florida, and without those votes, there would not have been a need for a recount in that state because Al Gore would have clearly won the election. "George W. Bush should thank Florida Muslims for opening his way to the White House," wrote Findley. Whether or not Al Gore would have been more favorable to Muslims is something that only Allah knows, and therefore Muslims should learn what they can from the 2000 election experience and move on.

Machine Politics

During the 1960s and early 1970s, the Democratic Party in Chicago was under the leadership of the late Mayor Richard J. Daley, father of current Mayor Richard M. Daley. What Daley did is without a doubt the greatest model of **machine politics** in the history of politics itself. The word "machine" comes from the way the Democratic Party under Daley functioned and the way he ran it. He was the operator, the party organization was the engine, and the sweat of thousands of party activists who were usually city employees provided the fuel for the engine. Together, this great machine produced votes, in every election, for whoever the party leadership wanted to elect.

"Old Man" Daley controlled the central committee of the Democratic Party. This committee slated people for public office. The committeemen of each of the city's 50 wards, or districts, would then do the work on the ground to get those who were chosen elected, as well as to get those who faithfully served the party through their roles as elected officials re-elected. The **precinct captains** went door-to-door with sheets in their hands to check off whose votes they had. Because of the primaries election system and Illinois law, the party that a person votes for, as well as whether or not that person voted in any particular election, is public information, so the precinct captain would look for the names with the big "D" next to them and stop; if there was an "R" he would probably move on. In those days, if people needed things done, they told their precinct captain. He would in turn tell the ward boss, who would for example, write a letter to the telephone company demanding that they take care of a problem that an old lady was having with her phone, write a letter to the police department in support of their accepting a young man from the neighborhood to join the force, settle disputes between neighbors, and even give money to needy families who were too ashamed to go on welfare. In return for the help they provided, the precinct captains and the ward bosses expected, or even demanded, that those who were helped return the favor by voting on Election Day. The voting sheets showed who voted and who did not vote, so if someone got help from the ward organization and did not return the favor, that would probably be the last bit of help they ever got. In those days, the system was so solid and the political corruption so widespread, that you usually had to know somebody to get something done or to get a job. That somebody was usually the precinct captain. In Arabic, the title of such a person would be a *wasta*, or connector, bridging the person that has a problem with the person who can solve that problem.

The precinct captains were never paid, directly that is. Their incentive for volunteering was simple-if they did so, they would keep their nice day job with the city; if not, then the ward boss would easily replace him with any one of dozens of men who wanted both jobs. Daley used thousands of city workers as his own political army to make sure that he got the right people elected who would help him with his agenda for the city. As long as everyone did their part and got the votes out on Election Day, then the system would stay in place and every member of the machine would benefit. If the machine were to break down, which it never did, then people would lose their jobs and would never work for the city again--it was as simple as that.

The machine has virtually changed, as election laws and public opinion about politics has changed. The effectiveness of the hardworking precinct captain has been replaced by TV commercials and campaign literature sent in the mail. In Chicago, as well as in other machine-run cities like New York and Philadelphia, the whole mood of politics has changed. The machine has become obsolete, or too old, to be effective. Many parts of the machine live on in American politics, some good, like volunteers going door to door, and some bad, like the *wasta*-style corruption. Campaigns are now run more systematically and, as many complain, less personally. Wealthy candidates try to meet their constituents in their living rooms through their TV screens, instead of meeting them in person. Unfortunately, too many Americans buy into this impersonal solicitation of votes and support the candidate who has the best commercial. Those frustrated with this and other negative aspects of campaigns that allow those who spend the most to win have been pushing for what is known as **campaign finance reform.**

Through new laws and the amending of existing ones, campaign finance reforms would take much of the emphasis off of fundraising for candidates so that they could base their campaigns on solid issues, without worrying about how to raise millions. This would give those who do not have their own personal wealth to run a campaign the opportunity to compete on an even level with wealthy candidates, and it would free candidates from the controls that interests groups have on them through campaign contributions. For Muslims, this issue should be a priority because the pro-Israel lobby spends millions of dollars each year on campaign contributions. Politicians in turn support the pro-Israel agenda in Congress. Limitations on those contributions, or even a ban on them, would free many politicians from the hold of lobbyists, and thus American foreign policy may very well become balanced in the Muslim World.

The Electoral College

In every election in the country, except for one, the people **directly elect** candidates to office. The only exception is the presidential election. People do vote for a president, but those votes do not directly determine who will win the election. Instead of the direct election of the president, the American political system has the indirect system known as the **Electoral College**. Each state elects delegates to the college based on the number of congressmen and senators that represent them in Washington. The District of Columbia (Washington, DC) also elects three delegates, so there are a total of 538 members in the electoral college. The candidate that gets the most popular votes in a state gets all of the **electoral votes**. This principal is known as "winner take all." A candidate needs a majority of at least 270 electoral votes to win the presidency. Therefore, candidates campaign most in the states with the largest number of votes like California,

Michigan, Florida, and New York. States like Montana and Hawaii, with only a few electoral votes, are pretty much ignored during presidential campaigns because attention is focused on the states that will win the election.

George W. Bush isn't the only president who lost the popular vote and still won enough electoral votes to become president. Similar circumstances won the presidency for John Quincy Adams in 1824, Rutherford B. Hayes in 1876, and Benjamin Harrison in 1888.

Again, going back to the 2000 presidential elections, Al Gore had over a half a million more votes than George Bush in the popular vote, but he still lost the election because Bush, having won Florida, received a majority of electoral votes.

Table 6: Results of 2000 Presidential Election

Candidate	Popular Vote	Electoral Votes
Gore	50,996,116	267
Bush	50,456,169	271
Other	3,874,040	0
Total:	105,326,325	538

Although Gore got 539,947 more votes than Bush across the country, Bush got 4 more electoral votes, winning him the presidency.

The candidate who wins the race in November becomes the president-elect. He begins a transition into the White House, while the outgoing president remains in power for a couple more months. For the outgoing president, the transition period after the election is known as the **Lame Duck season**, for time is almost up. People are looking forward to the new president who will be inaugurated, or take office on January 20th of the upcoming year. That date has been fixed by law.

About two weeks before the inauguration, Congress will come into session where the members of the Electoral College will cast their votes on behalf of their states. This is a ceremonial process because the outcome is already known. Some delegates in the past have revolted and cast their vote for the opposing candidate, but most states have laws now to ensure than such things do not happen. The political parties make sure that they do not have any rebels representing their state in the Electoral College.

In the event that no one candidate receives a majority of electoral votes, an election is held by the House of Representatives, with each state having one vote. The winner of that contest well then become president. Also, the Senate would be the body that picks a vice president if none of the candidates received a majority of electoral votes.

DID YOU KNOW?

Former Washington, DC mayor Marion Barry served three terms in office before he went to jail in 1990 after the FBI videotaped him smoking crack cocaine in a hotel room. He served six months in prison for drug possession. In 1994 the voters of Washington, DC elected Barry to another term as mayor.

CHAPTER 9

INTEREST GROUPS

The decisions of politicians on whether or not to support certain issues are often influenced by **interest groups**, or groups whose members have the same concerns about issues. Interest groups can have as few as 20 people or as many as two million, and they can be local, national, or both. The strategy of the interest group is to take all of the influence that individual members have and pool it together to maximize that influence for the sake of the interests of the group.

There are over 7,000 such organizations registered in Washington, DC. These interest groups are there to be close to elected officials and bureaucrats, or government workers in charge of implementing programs and making and overseeing regulations, or rules. An interest group can also be called a lobby. One who works on behalf of an interest group is a lobbyist. This term is not that pleasant, however, to many Americans because they associate lobbyists with the buying of influence through campaign contributions and gifts, like free vacations and basketball tickets. Despite this negative image, lobbyists continue to be major players in the decision-making process. Many lobbyists are actually former elected officials who use their experience and contacts in government in order to benefit the issue they're hired to work on.

Types of Interest Groups

Public interest groups are concerned with issues that are related to the community or society in general. The goal of these groups is to promote their vision for making certain aspects of life better for Americans. The **Sierra Club,** for example, works to protect the environment from pollution and commercial development. They try to stop the wood industry, for instance, from cutting down trees in forests that are home to thousands of species of animals. Another very popular interest group is **Common Cause**, an organization dedicated to making government more efficient. Campaign finance reform is perhaps the most important issue promoted by Common Cause.

Economic interest groups are concerned with money: how much money their members will get, when and how, either directly or indirectly, through government contracts or government policies that will be good for the business of the members of the interest group. There are more economic interest groups than any other type in Washington. These lobbies are often trade groups that represent entire industries. For example, the **AFL-CIO** and the **International Brotherhood of Teamsters** represent most labor unions in the country. The interests of physicians are represented by the **American Medical Association (AMA)**. The **U.S. Chamber of Commerce** is probably the most diverse trade group, and one of the most influential as well, promoting the welfare of American business.

Local and state governments have their own interest groups as well. **Government** interest groups may represent hundreds or thousands of the same type of jurisdiction. For instance, the mayors of American cities have the **National**

Conference of Mayors to represent their interests in Washington. There are others like the **National Governors Association** and the **National Association of Counties**. Such groups are needed because of the nature of the system. Each layer of government is responsible for its own maintenance and functioning. Therefore there is always internal competition between various jurisdictions at the local, state, and national level. Remember, everyone wants the biggest piece of the federal government's pie that they can get.

Civil Rights interest groups are well known for trying to influence government policies in order to benefit minorities, women, and immigrants. These interest groups are usually grassroots, meaning that their membership comes straight from the ground to work together for the common issue that unites them. The most popular civil rights group in the country is the **National Association for the Advancement of Colored People (NAACP)**. The NAACP has been behind the civil rights movement since it gained momentum in the 1950s. **CAIR** is the Muslim equivalent to the NAACP. Many may think that these organizations are not interest groups, but indeed they are, for the common interest of their members is that their civil rights be honored and they take that message to policymakers in Washington and elsewhere.

Part of the challenge for civil rights groups is first, educating community members about the rights that they have under the law, and second, making them care enough to do something when these rights are violated by individuals, groups, or even the government. For many immigrant Muslims, the idea of standing up to the government when it is wrong is scary because in the countries that they were born in, such activity could get them arrested or even killed. So long as they and their families are safe and unbothered, they may not care so much about their rights to privacy, or freedom of association.

Islamic civil rights groups are helping to change this mentality by proving that standing up to injustice and struggling is the only way to protect the rights and liberties of Muslims in America.

Single-Issue interest groups are only concerned about one issue. The **National Rifle Association (NRA)** is the most powerful lobby in Washington. The NRA promotes the rights of law-abiding citizens to own guns without restrictions from the government. The NRA bases its argument on the 2nd Amendment of the U.S. Constitution, which gives citizens the right to bear arms (own weapons). The NRA has an estimated 2.5 million members, who are predominantly Republican and very vocal. The **National Coalition to Ban Handguns (NCBH)** is also a single-issue lobby. It fights for controls on the sale of weapons and for the limiting of the amount, and types, of weapons that citizens can own. The NCBH also uses the 2nd Amendment for their argument saying that the NRA deceives people because they do not recite the rest of the 2nd Amendment, which states that the right to bear arms is given to those to establish a state militia. The term militia was relevant when the Constitution was being drafted because the regular army was weak, and it depended on citizen militias for help if war were to break out. NCBH argues that now with a strong army, militias are not needed, and therefore the right to bear arms does not apply to just anyone who wants to own guns.

Another example of single-issue interest groups are those who advocate for abortion rights, like the **National Abortion**

Rights Action League (NARAL), and, on the flip side, the National Right to Life Committee (NRLC), which lobbies for the banning of abortions. Single-issue interest groups draw people who are passionate about such issues, and often bring out the best in American democracy by mobilizing people into action to express themselves, openly and freely.

The Function of Interest Groups

Interest groups have several functions in politics. They represent the collective opinions of their members on their issues. They lobby, or fight, for policies that are favorable to their issues, they educate policymakers and the public in general about their issues, and they serve as a source of information for politicians, government regulators, the general public, and their own members as well.

The members, whether they are people, businesses, unions, or municipalities, give interest groups the right to represent their positions on issues of importance to them. The leaders of these interest groups then take their positions to those in government who can get the job done. The **California Strawberry Growers Association** is not going to waste its time by going to the chairman of the House Armed Services Committee to try to get help for strawberry farmers who have lost crops because of a drought in California. Obviously, they would be directing their attention to the chairman and other influential members of the **House Agriculture Committee**, the **Farm Credit Administration**, and the **Food and Drug Administration (FDA)**, since these are the bodies that have the power to deal with their issue. The government may even take the first step by contacting the association and offering help because they know that such an association for strawberry growers in California exists.

Therefore interest groups are not always just bugging politicians to help them out. On the contrary, they play a key role in connecting the government with the sentiments of the people. The relationship between Congress, the federal government, and interest groups is known as the **Iron Triangle.** Critics of the Iron Triangle argue that larger interest groups dominate in such a climate, and that interest groups act as if public opinion supports their positions, when in reality, it may only be their members who are supporting them.

Lobbyists know that only half of their job is meeting with officials to gain support for their issues. Another part of lobbying deals with writing potential legislation that a member of Congress can introduce if he/she is interested enough to do so. A good amount of legislation that passes through Congress originates not in the sponsoring congressman's office, but in the office of lobbyists who work for interest groups. Also, interest groups do research and gather statistics and other information that they present to congressmen and senators on a regular basis. Those members of Congress often use that information during speeches or while in committee hearings. Lobbyists themselves often appear in hearings to present their positions directly to members of Congress.

Finally, interest groups have the function of being a source of information to the government as a whole and to the general public. The **Dairy Council** runs television ads that ask "Got Milk?" The **Mexican-American Legal Defense and Education Fund (MALDEF)** may run radio ads that highlight the heritage and culture of Latinos in this country. The **American Automobile Association (AAA)** may hold seminars at local community centers to offer tips on car seat safety.

After 9/11, several Muslim-American organizations took out full-page ads in major newspapers in order to condemn the terrorist attacks and to assure readers that their Muslim neighbors are as patriotic as all other Americans. In response to the ads, those organizations were contacted by people and government officials for more information.

Indeed, interests groups in this regard have an opportunity to educate people about who they are, what they do, and what issues they stand for.

Lobbying

When interest groups want something, they lobby for it. Lobbyists understand that politicians want to know two things: how many people support their issue and how strongly do those people feel about that issue? The more support that groups have for an issue, the more influence they will have with policymakers. The challenge for lobbyists is to demonstrate to an official that the positions presented are not the views of one person, but of hundreds, or thousands, or even millions. The lobbyist also knows that if none of the people whom he represents lives in the district or state of the official whom he is meeting with, then the official will not feel much pressure to give the lobbyist what he/she wants.

It takes a very powerful person or group to walk into a congressman's office and say "support our issue or else...." Since most lobbyists do not have such clout, they take a more diplomatic approach, presenting their position clearly with information and statistics to back up their argument. They explain to the politician how supporting an issue will help his district or state and how it will help him politically. Here, the lobbyist offers votes and/or money to the politician who will eventually run for office again unless he retires. Money is important, but votes are more important. Muslims and

Arabs may not give much money to John Dingell (D-MI), but then again they really do not have to because Congressman Dingell represents Dearborn, Michigan, and the Muslims and Arabs in that area have tens of thousands of votes to offer. It is no surprise then that Dingell is very supportive of Muslim concerns. He may sincerely care about the Muslim community and their issues, but their votes give him the political incentive to support them even if his heart does not.

When a vote is scheduled for a bill that is important to an interest group with a grassroots membership, they may send out an **"Action Alert"** through faxes and emails, telling members to call their congressman or senators and demand that they vote a certain way on the upcoming bill. This is a very effective tool, especially if a group can get many people to call their own representative or senator, as opposed to just any member of Congress. When that person in the Washington or district office answers a call from a constituent, he will handle it more carefully and count it separately from other calls because it comes from a constituent. If 50 constituents called a congressman's office in one day demanding that he/she votes a certain way, then that congressman will probably do so because he knows that for every person who takes the time to call Washington long distance, there are probably hundreds who have not called but who feel the same way. If a person is not a constituent, then his/her call is virtually meaningless, if not annoying, to the staffers who answer the phones and writes down the comments of constituents.

If an issue is less timely, let's say something to do with policy in general, but not to a specific bill, interest groups may ask their members to write letters to their elected officials asking that something be done about the problem at hand. A large amount of letters from constituents are more important than phone calls because anyone who takes the time to write a letter is surely someone who takes the time to vote.

If a politician is not responsive to the interest group, a demonstration may be held in front of that politician's office, which is likely to draw the media and undoubtedly bad press for that politician. If a politician totally ignores an interest group, that group may work with the politician's opponent in the upcoming elections to help get him out of office. This is true for any office. For those interest groups that work on the local level, and are made up of volunteers, knowing how to approach politicians and maintaining good relations with them and their staff is important. Picking someone with a strong accent to speak on behalf of a group is not a wise decision if there are equally qualified people in the group--even if they are younger--who are American-born and speak without an accent. There are many reasons for this, the main one being: if people do not understand what you are saying, then they don't care about what you are saying. This is why the training of young Muslims is important because it helps in the communication process. It also changes the perception of Muslims in the eyes of other citizens from being a population of foreigners to a religious community that is part of the American fabric.

The above lesson cannot be applied, however, if groups are complaining about policies but not reaching out to politicians to express their opinions. Simply put, if you are not talking to a politician, it is impossible for him or her to listen to you. When approached by Muslims in Washington, many congressmen and senators complain that they do not know who the Muslims are in their districts and states, and that they would love to meet with them if they did. So those who have not done so should identify who their elected officials are, and then call their offices to request meetings with them. Even if there is not an immediate issue of concern, it is good to establish relations with politicians because it will benefit the group in the long run. If a politician cares about keeping the support of a group, he or she will work for their issues and may also work to get money for programs in their communities. A Muslim community center may get a grant of $100,000 to fund an after-school program for neighborhood youth with the help of the local congressman. In return, that congressman will count on the Muslims to vote for him in the next election. Again, this is an example of *quid pro quo*.

Groups should not get too attached to politicians however. Friendly relations are good, but relationships should remain professional. The politician should never be allowed to feel that he or she has done enough for your group. A famous saying on Capitol Hill goes: "There are no permanent friends in politics, nor are there permanent enemies; there are only permanent issues."

Political Action Committees

A **Political Action Committee**, or **PAC**, is an organization that raises money, and then distributes that money to candidates. PACs are either independent or they are related to interest groups or corporations that are limited, by law, in their political activity. Whereas an individual can give only $2,000 to a candidate running for the Senate, let's say, a PAC can give up to $5,000. PACs usually give their money to incumbents, or those who already hold office because they want to encourage government policies that are good for their interests.

According to the Federal Elections Commission, there were 3,868 federally registered PACs across America at the beginning of 2004. This is a great increase from 1974, when there were only 608 registered PACs in the United States. The largest number of PACs ever to operate at one time was 4,268 back in 1988.

PACs are regulated by the government. They must file reports on who gives them money, and how much, as well as to whom they give money and how much. The PAC has been the secret behind the power of the pro-Israel lobby in the United States. One PAC alone may have a little influence with its $5,000 maximum contribution to a single candidate, but imagine if there were 10, or 20, or 50 PAC's that all had the same agenda, and gave their money to the same people with the same message. This is what the pro-Israel lobby has done. At one time, there were over 70 PACs in Washington, DC lobbying Congress on behalf of Israel. In his book *Stealth PAC's*, Richard Curtiss, the executive editor of the *Washington Report on Middle East Affairs* magazine, describes how these pro-Israel PAC's worked together, under the guidance of AIPAC, to successfully win the support of Congress time and again for Israel. Curtiss points out that most of these PACs do not have obvious names with the words "Israel" or "Jewish" in them. This is intentional so that their lobbying efforts are made more secret.

The number of these pro-Israel PACs has decreased in recent years, and the number of Muslim PACs has increased. There are fewer then a dozen Muslim and Arab PACs in the

United States, but their numbers will certainly grow as Muslim and Arab-Americans become more politically savvy. The effectiveness of PACs, however, may not be so powerful in the near future if Congress continues to pass campaign reform bills that take away excessive influence from wealthy individuals and organizations.

Until then, Muslims should form PACs. The best way to do this is for a group of people to get together and commit anywhere from $1,000 to $5,000 every year to a PAC. Once commitments are made, a lawyer with relevant experience should be consulted to make sure that the proper procedures are followed, including FEC registration and reporting, opening of bank accounts, and so forth. Once all of the technical obstacles are out of the way, all of those who committed should contribute their money to the PAC and elect a board to oversee its operations. The person who heads the board should be the only one to speak on behalf of the group when meeting with elected officials and this person should present the members of the PAC with recommendations of whom they should contribute money to and why.

Figure 3: Model for Political Success

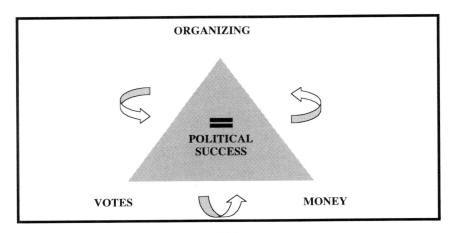

PACs can play an important role in building local blocks of Muslim voters by researching candidates for state, county, and city-wide elections, and then endorsing the candidates whom they determine deserve the community's support.

In the state of Virginia, several Muslim activists established the **Platform for Active Civil Empowerment (PACE)**, which is a statewide PAC that endorses candidates and distributes political contributions to those candidates. PACE was established after 9/11 as a vehicle for local Muslims to organize politically in order to fight discrimination and promote justice. Its focus on local politics has been very successful.

Afeefa Syeed, a PACE board member and founder of Al-Fatih Academy in Loudoun County, VA, took local political involvement to the next level when she ran for and won the Democratic nomination for a seat on the County Board of Supervisors. When Election Day rolled around, however, she lost. Still, she and the hundreds of community members who supported her were very happy to have had the opportunity to gain first-hand experience in the political process, which will undoubtedly help them in the future.

DID YOU KNOW?

According to Fortune Magazine, the five most powerful lobbying groups in Washington, DC are:

1. National Rifle Association-NRA

2. American Association of Retired Persons-AARP

3. National Federation of Independent Business-NFIB

4. American-Israel Public Affairs Committee-AIPAC

5. Association of Trial Lawyers of America-ATLA

CHAPTER 10

PRACTICAL STEPS TO TAKE

In order to encourage people to get involved in politics and government, some guidance is required on practical steps they can take to put words and ideas into action. This chapter will offer such advice and effective techniques for individuals, communities, and youth who have a desire to take action for the sake of the greater good. Many of the skills in this chapter have been taught to hundreds of Muslim activists through seminars during a 15-month training tour across America by the MAS Freedom Foundation.

Lobbying: Anybody Can Do It!

Individuals who want to make a difference in society often become advocates for certain causes. They carry out certain actions in order to influence decision makers on public policy issues. It doesn't take a degree in political science to become a good Muslim advocate. The only requirements are sincerity, commitment, and determination. Like anything else in life, you win some and you lose some, but you should never quit if you want to succeed.

Earlier we discussed how interest groups lobby, or advocate, for policies that benefit their issues. Remember, politics is a series of relationships that determines who gets what, when, and how. Who gets the income, education, housing, health-care, and justice is determined by policies that are fostered by political relationships. When you lobby your elected officials, you are building relationships with them based on trust and mutual interests, with the goal of getting better public policy.

Now we will discuss the path, from beginning to end, that any individual can take in order to successfully lobby public officials. Groups of individuals can also study this path for collective lobbying.

WHAT'S YOUR PROBLEM?

Identify what issues concern you, not just as a Muslim, but as a member of society. Before you can be an effective advocate, you must educate yourself about the issues. Take out a piece of paper and write down the issues that you are concerned about: civil liberties, foreign policy, high property taxes, same-sex marriage, a proposed bill to legalize gambling, crime, etc. Your issues can be both positive and negative. Don't just think about what you would complain about, also think about good things that can be done. This might be hard for many people who have isolated themselves in the Muslim community. Such individuals should think about their daily lives and about what upsets them. Those potholes on your street that are ruining you car, that big chunk of money that the government takes out of your check on payday, that homeless person you see everyday sleeping in the park, and so on are just some issues that concern many.

Narrow down the list to those issues that make you so upset that you are willing to do something about them. Thus you have your own portfolio of public policy issues of concern. Take the top issue and start from there.

Now that you have an issue for which you want to lobby, start your research. Don't rely on your general knowledge of the issue. Do an objective search to find out all of the arguments for and against the issue, or the different opinions on how to solve a specific problem. Find out who is behind the various positions.

Once you do your research, you can develop an informed opinion on the subject at hand, and you should have a clear idea of what your objectives are. For example, if your issue was homelessness, you would have found out how many homeless people live in the area, what government programs are in place to assist them, how effective these programs are, what does not work with these programs, and who is proposing what new solutions to the homeless problem? Then you might come to the conclusion that the government needs to provide more shelters to get the homeless off the street. This would be your objective, and this is what you would want the government to do.

WHO DO I TALK TO?

Determine if your issue is a local, state, or federal issue. You wouldn't call your congressman in Washington to complain about high property taxes. Your congressman deals with federal issues, and property taxes are a local issue. Similarly, you wouldn't call your governor to complain about the war on Iraq because your governor deals only with issues in his/her state. The war is a foreign policy matter dealt with at the national level. The worksheet in Appendix I will help you identify who your elected officials are at all levels of government.

If you don't know who to talk to, simply call the office that you think might be able to help and ask them, "Can you help me with this issue, and if not, can you please tell me who can?" People usually are very helpful. If you called the Department of Housing and Urban Development (HUD) in Washington and explained that you needed help with the homelessness problem in your area, the person on the other line either would tell you how HUD could help, or he/she would tell you that you probably need to call your state senator or representative, or maybe even the mayor's office.

You wouldn't want to just talk to someone on the phone though about such an important issue. You'd want to have a meeting in order to advocate on behalf of your issue.

ARRANGING A MEETING

Call and ask for a meeting. Now that you are about to start contacting people, you want to think about who is on your side in the community. When you eventually meet with public officials, it is preferable for you to take a small group of people who will back you up on your issues. You can join an established group, start a new group and attract supporters, or you can be the facilitator that brings interested individuals like yourself together for a specific purpose.

If you don't have the phone number of the office with which you wish to arrange a meeting, try looking in the White Pages, on the Internet, or call 411 for the phone number. Call and ask to speak with the scheduler. Identify yourself and the purpose of your phone call. It helps to be speaking on behalf of a group or institution—just make sure you have permission to do so before you call. If you are calling as an individual, just tell them that you are calling on behalf of a group of concerned citizens or constituents.

Be courteous on the phone and be flexible with the scheduling. Remember, you are the one trying to get a slot in the schedule of a very busy person. Often, you will be asked to meet with a member of the staff of that politician, which is fine. Meeting with the staff is almost as important as, and sometimes more important than, meeting with the actual principal or main figure. In the case of the homelessness problem, you may call the mayor's office and be told that you can meet with his/her deputy for housing affairs. The deputy is the one who will report to his/her principal the outcome of his/her meeting with you and make recommendations. The principal, in this case the mayor, does not have time to get bogged down with details. He/she makes decisions, to a great extent, based on the recommendations of his/her staff.

Many times, public offices will ask that you fax them a formal letter requesting a meeting. You should comply and fax your letter as soon as possible so that there is no delay. Sometimes, hurdles are intentionally put in your way in order for the office to determine if you are someone who means business or someone who is going to waste their time.

By now you have called, and maybe even faxed a letter requesting a meeting. Then you get a call back with good news—the mayor and his/her housing deputy will meet with you for 20 minutes. Some meetings are even shorter than that. Rarely do meetings with principals go past half an hour.

THE BIG DAY

Your meeting delegation should consist of 2 to 5 people. You don't want to go to the meeting by yourself, because it will send a signal that you are alone on this issue. At the same time, you don't want to take too many people with you, because there are probably not enough chairs in the room for everyone to sit down. Also, having too many people present will be a distraction, especially if everyone is trying to speak at the same time.

When identifying those you want to take with you, think of the role that they can play and of their potential influence on the mayor and his/her staff. Let's assume that you will represent your local mosque on this issue, in addition to being the spokesperson for the entire group. You might want to take with you a minister or a rabbi who can talk about their first-hand experience in dealing with the homeless, a lawyer to discuss legal or legislative aspects of possible solutions, an advocate from a homeless rights group or some other civic organization, and a young person from the Muslim community who can learn from the process, while at the same time taking notes during the meeting and keeping track of time.

Try to assemble your group before the meeting so that you can agree on the roles that everyone will play and on what each person will say. Create talking points, or key ideas that you want to express at the meeting. This really helps the meeting flow smoothly, and prevents one person from hogging up all the time and not letting others speak. The facilitator's goal should be to move things along according to schedule, but not to dictate things to others.

It is strongly recommended that you have detailed written information to present to the mayor and his staff at the meeting, as it will be helpful to them in the follow-up stage. Try to have statistics from credible sources so that they don't have to just take your word for it, which they probably won't anyway.

Furthermore, through the talking points or information handouts, you want to be able to address the four questions that every politician asks him/herself in the back of his/her mind: 1) Does this make sense?, 2) How does this affect my city/district/state?, 3) Will it help or hurt me politically?, and 4) Does anyone else know or care about this issue?

Dress professionally for the meeting, and make sure to shut off your cell phone or pager before entering the office. Plan to arrive 15 minutes early so that you give yourself room for unexpected delays or difficulties in parking.

Be friendly to everyone you encounter from the time you walk into the office until the time you walk out of the office. Remember, the staff members usually are the ones who do the detailed work on your issues and give advice to the principal, so you want to be sure to make a good impression on everyone.

Introduce yourself to the mayor and any of his/her staff that are present, and then introduce your colleagues. If you have an accent, speak slowly and clearly so that you are understood. You should be pleasant and friendly. But remember, you are there for business and you are meeting with someone who was elected by the people, so don't waste a lot of time thanking the mayor for meeting with you and flattering him with a bunch of praise.

A word of caution here about shaking hands. Many Muslims do not feeling comfortable shaking hands with members of the opposite sex for religious reasons, while others have no problem with it at all. It can be very awkward to have one Muslim woman shake hands with Mr. Mayor, while another Muslim woman in the same group does not. Sometimes people decide on the spot and then immediately change their mind, i.e. they will stick their hand out slightly forward and then pull it back.

If this is an issue for you, the best way to handle it is for you to decide ahead of time if you will shake hands or not. If you walk into the room and a member of the opposite sex is there and ready to shake your hand, but you do not want to do so, simply smile, put your hand across your heart, and give a little "Japanese" bow as you say, "I'm sorry, but for religious reasons I do not shake hands with members of the opposite sex." The smile and bow help, and the other person will probably apologize for almost insulting you, and bow back.

As the facilitator, you should have a notepad with the objectives of your group and the talking points written down to refer to throughout the meeting. The clock is ticking, so you need to stay focused and stick to your talking points. Don't be greedy by trying to talk about several public policy issues at one time, turning the meeting into a therapy session where the principal listens to you talk your heart out with his hand on his chin, as he nods every so often before thanking you for coming. You walk out of the meeting feeling great about having the politician's ear, while in reality your meeting was a failure.

Just as you do not want to go off on a tangent, you have to guard yourself from the politician who will try to discuss tangential issues in order to avoid addressing your concerns. Try to bring the conversation back to the issue at hand by saying something like, "Well that's great, but we know you are busy so we'd like to come back to the issue of homelessness if we may." Just don't ever cut other people off or try to speak over them, as that is very rude.

Remember, you are there because there is a problem, and either you have an idea for solving it or you want to know what your elected official is going to do about it.

In the end, the politician may promise to study the issue, or direct his/her staff to work with you further. Whatever the commitment, make sure that you immediately establish a mechanism for follow-up by saying something like, "So should we call you next week to follow up?" Also ask if there is anything that you can do in the meantime.

Once the mechanism for follow-up is worked out, the meeting is over, and you make your way out. The end of the meeting should be just that—the end, not the beginning to discuss another topic. There will be plenty of time in the future to discuss other issues with politicians and their staff if you plan on staying active. It is important to keep in mind that you are establishing a relationship with these people, one that can last a long time. So be patient, and think strategically about your approach to these relationships.

After the meeting, it is a good idea to draft a letter that summarizes what was discussed in the meeting, including any commitments and follow-up mechanisms. Fax this letter to the politician's office. Keeping a paper trail, or documentation, can be very valuable when disagreements arise about who was supposed to do what and when. And remember, it's your job to follow up.

Join a Party and Work on Campaigns

If you ask many political activists and politicians how they first got involved in politics, a large number of them will undoubtedly say that they joined a political party and volunteered for a campaign.

If you know with which party you identify more, call up their local office and tell them that you want to volunteer.

They will be very glad to have you, as volunteers provide free labor. If it is an election year you may be assigned to a campaign. You will be used for the talents or potential that you possess. Volunteers usually start out by putting up signs and knocking on people's doors to gather support for their candidate, but campaign managers are quick to notice your skills and ambition and maximize them for the sake of getting the candidate elected or re-elected, so you may get promoted quickly.

As a Muslim, you might find yourself doing ethnic outreach. If you are a college student or recent graduate, you might be dispatched to college campuses and places where young adults hang out in order to register them to vote, hopefully winning their support for your candidate in the process.

If elected, your candidate will probably hire most of his staff from those who worked on his campaign, both employees and volunteers. You might get a job out of it or you might be appointed to some position that your candidate now has the power to fill. This is called patronage: your candidate is your patron and you are his/her loyal foot soldier who may get rewarded with a job.

Even if your candidate loses, you will have gained a tremendous amount of experience on the campaign. Also, you still will be a party activist who will be needed for other campaigns. You will have met leaders and future leaders, and you will have hopefully presented a positive image of Muslims through your ethics and behavior.

Joining a political party is crucial for those who wish to run for office one day or receive political appointments to government jobs. Party members are the ones chosen as delegates to the national party conventions every four years, where the platforms for each party are voted on. The opportunities are plenty.

A bit of advice to Muslims who may be candidates for office themselves one day. Run your campaign as a candidate who happens to be Muslim, rather than "the Muslim candidate." If you run as the Muslim candidate, you will appear as an outsider to the larger electorate, and you will be held to a very high standard by the Muslim community when you meet with them to seek their support. A Muslim lawyer running for a state Senate seat was quoted in the local newspaper as saying that he doesn't always pray five times a day. When he turned to the local mosque for support, community members ridiculed him for not being an exemplary Muslim. His reaction was to label his community as a bunch of extremists. So beware of pandering to your own community for their support, or allowing them to expect the world from you because it may backfire on you.

Candidates' Forums and Evaluations

Muslim voters often express their frustration with the notion of being encouraged to register to vote but not being informed of which candidates the Muslim community supports outside of the presidential contest.

The best way to determine who deserves the Muslim vote in your community is by holding candidate forums—an opportunity to invite candidates running for different offices to address community members. Another way is to send candidates questionnaires that ask for their positions on issues of interest to the Muslim community.

Individuals alone cannot do this work effectively. It is recommended that an independent committee be established for the purpose of endorsing candidates for office. The committee's first task should be to determine with which issues the Muslim community is most concerned. The committee should then come to a representative conclusion on what its policy agenda should be.

Next, the committee should publicize its existence to the community and create a mechanism for individuals to offer constructive input into the endorsement process. It is important for community members to have their voices heard and know that this body represents their interests.

Once the committee and its legitimacy are established, a list of candidates running for office should be obtained from the local elections board. You can find their phone number online, in the phone book, or by calling 411. Questionnaires should be drawn up for candidates of various offices and then mailed or faxed to their campaign headquarters. Make sure that an explanation of who the committee represents is on the questionnaire, as well as contact information. Larger campaigns may prefer that questionnaires be sent via e-mail.

Some sample questions that you might include in a questionnaire are:

1. What is your stance on the USA PATRIOT Act?

2. How do you plan to fight religious discrimination?

3. What is your immigration policy?

4. What is your stance on same-sex marriage?

5. What is your position on abortion?

6. How do you plan to solve the homeless problem?

Upon receiving the responses, the committee should evaluate each candidate based on their positions on critical issues facing the community, their history with the community (if any), their integrity and professional qualifications, and their electability.

To enhance the evaluation process, the local mosque or community center can host an open candidates' forum, in which all candidates running for specific offices are invited and offered two minutes to address your voters. Mosques should check with their lawyers to ensure that guidelines are in place to protect the mosque from partisan political activity being conducted in its name. Religious institutions that are classified as 501(c)(3) organizations by the IRS cannot suggest to their worshippers who they should vote for or which party they should join. As long as the rules against favoring one candidate or party over another are followed, mosques can participate in the political process. Mosques can even distribute scorecards that rate the performance and positions of incumbents and challengers.

The candidates' forum should be scheduled at least three weeks in advance to give you time to publicize the event in the community, and to give candidates the time to work it into their schedules. As for the event itself, a moderator should open the event and introduce the speakers and candidates. Avoid long speeches by community leaders as this event is meant for the community to hear from the candidates.

The committee that was set up to evaluate candidates for endorsement should now have all of the information needed in order to choose the list of candidates, if any, that deserve the Muslim vote. The endorsements should be put together in a flier or pamphlet and distributed to as many Muslim voters as possible anywhere from two to four weeks before the election. The committee should also send the endorsements to the candidates that they have selected to inform them of the support that they can expect from their Muslim constituents.

If the committee comes across outstanding candidates that deserve support, it may recruit volunteers from the community in order to work on that candidate's campaign. As Election Day nears, the committee must work hard to remind Muslims to go out and vote for the candidates that they endorsed.

After the election, a report should be prepared to track the outcome of the races in which the committee endorsed candidates, as well as the margins of victory. Those endorsed candidates who won their election should be listed on the report and distributed to the community as well as to the candidate's campaign in order to remind everybody that the Muslim community had a role in the victory of the candidates that were endorsed by the committee.

Building Coalitions

Having a strong community-based organization to represent the political interests of the Muslim community is very good, but having non-Muslim organizations fighting for your issues is superb. Other groups will be willing to help you on your issues if you are willing to help them on theirs. What's more, your interests on some issue may overlap. This is the formula for a coalition.

Coalitions, or alliances, are interesting phenomena. Groups that would be working in different fields, or even against each other on one issue, may find themselves side by side on another issue.

Case in point: the issue of gambling in the state of Maryland. In 2003, Governor Robert Ehrlich introduced a plan to bring thousands of slots machines to the state in order to generate money to fill a hole in the state's budget. A coalition was formed by religious, civic, and business groups to fight the governor's attempts to legalize gambling in Maryland.

The MAS Freedom Foundation joined Christian groups from various denominations, the League of Women Voters, the restaurant association, and even the association that represents bars and liquor stores to establish the "Stop Slots Maryland Coalition." Many wondered how religious groups and the liquor lobby could work together when they are ideologically at odds, but that is the nature of politics. As stated earlier, there are no such things as permanent friends or permanent enemies, just permanent issues.

The coalition helped fight back the governor. His slots proposal was defeated in 2003, and again in 2004. The Muslims in the coalition were warmly welcomed by their allies. The author of this book along with his former colleague Mahdi Bray both testified before the Senate and House of Delegates, urging lawmakers to reject the gambling initiative.

Entering into a large coalition does not mean that you support the agendas or ideologies of the other groups in your alliance. Many Muslims found it difficult to work with some organizations in the anti-war movement because they feared that their joining forces against the war on Iraq would send a signal that Muslims approved of their liberal agenda. This can be dealt with by making it clear that although you have joined other groups in the coalition to tackle a specific issue, there are certain issues that you will not be supportive of, like abortion rights or same-sex marriage.

Youth Action

Although the youth are always touted as being the future of the community, rarely are they prepared for that future. It is essential for communities to involve their youth in real-life activities that will put them on the path to leadership, not just in the mosque but also in society at large.

Parents should encourage their children to enter into fields that are not just financially beneficial, but also beneficial to the community, such as political science, journalism, and education.

Graduates with degrees in political science can go off to law school, which is a stepping-stone for many politicians. Nearly half of the members of Congress have law degrees. Another option is using a degree in political science to join the federal workforce or civil service and starting a career that may eventually lead to a position where policy decisions are made on a daily basis. Politicians come and go every election, but the civil servants who make a career out of their public service are the ones who make government run.

A degree in journalism can help young Muslims enter a field that for too long has misrepresented Islam and has fostered negative stereotypes about Muslims. Muslims have much to offer in the fields of news reporting and analysis, and they have a built-in multicultural nature that gives them an edge in this ever-shrinking global village we call Earth.

A degree in education is very important for one very simple reason. School teachers have a profound impact on the lives of their students, especially in the early grades. Let's say there is a Muslim woman, Ms. Aisha, who wears hijab and is a third grade teacher. Her students love her as she helps them with their problems and cares for them like her own children. The impression that she leaves with her students will last them a lifetime and help defeat negative stereotypes that those children are exposed to as they grow older. When they think of Islam or Muslims, they will probably think of Ms. Aisha before they think of Osama bin Laden. This is the key to changing the image of Islam in America.

Young Muslims should not rely totally on their elders for guidance, however. Often, they will have to take matters into their own hands. As soon as they turn 18, they should register to vote. A great activity for youth to get involved in is volunteering to register other people to vote. They can do this through a political party or campaign, as mentioned earlier, or they can call their local elections office and offer their time. Again, the image of a Muslim volunteering to encourage a fellow American to vote leaves a positive image in the mind of people and helps defeat stereotypes. One cannot simply say that Muslims are nice, peaceful people, especially in the post-9/11 world. They must show others the beauty of themselves and their faith through action.

Also, there is a very important local role that the youth can play with regard to elections. Polling places hire judges on Election Day to make sure that everyone who votes is eligible and to assist people if they need help. These election judges not only perform a valuable service, but they also get paid, sometimes over $150 for a long day's work.

During the summer, high school and college students have the opportunity to take part in internships with the offices of public officials or other government agencies. These internships offer great exposure to politics and government functioning from the inside. What's more, one can meet the leaders of today and tomorrow while on these internships, and build a network of relationships that may pay off in the future.

The U.S. House of Representatives offers an exciting program for high school juniors who wish to spend a semester in Washington and in Congress as a Page, or a young person who provides support to members of the House. Pages are paid for their work. Transportation to and from Washington is also included. They must stay in a dorm for pages where they attend classes in the morning before they head off to the Capitol for their jobs as congressional assistants.

There are about 72 pages working each semester. To be considered for the job, an applicant must be sponsored by his/her congressman, so there is a great deal of competition. Still, the hassle of trying to become a page is well worth the opportunity. To get more information, visit http://clerk.house.gov, or call your local congressman's office and ask about the page program.

Another opportunity to get first-hand knowledge of the legislative process is to join a simulation of government if it is offered in high school or college. Many states have Model Government programs in which teams of students from around the state travel to their state capital and play the roles of legislators. They pass bills, debate issues, take votes—all in the same chambers as the real politicians.

There are other programs, such as the Model United Nations and the Model Arab League, that are popular at some schools as well. Such role playing gives near real-life exposure to what it is like to have a career in politics.

DID YOU KNOW?

That schools often give credit for internships and volunteering with campaigns or political parties?

CHAPTER 11

CONCLUSION

By this point in the book, readers may be overwhelmed with information. However, one should keep in mind that like anything else, it takes time to get a really good understanding of the ins and outs of a subject. With the topics of politics and government, it takes more than just reading. People must actually interact with the system that has the most impact on their daily lives. We already interact with the government when we pay our taxes, go to traffic court, and send letters out from the post office. We are conscious of these things because we are the ones giving in these instances. Many may not be aware of when they are on the receiving end, however, like when they drive on a street that was cleared of snow, or when they walk through a park that is kept clean and pretty, or even when they send their kids off to public school for seven hours a day. The government affects our lives in countless ways. Politics is what shapes the way that government gets involved in our lives. Those who are informed and understand this process are much more likely to influence it, and thus benefit from it.

The challenge for Muslims is to become informed members of society for the sake of influencing the system in order to benefit from it. *Insha'Allah*, this book has made you, the reader, a more informed person, whether you are an immigrant or a Muslim who was born here, a practicing Muslim, or a secular Muslim.

As the "new kids on the block," Muslims will continue to face challenges from society, but that should not be an excuse for people to stay away from politics and Muslim organizations. The organizations that function on behalf of Muslims in the political arena work hard for the benefit of the community. They may make mistakes, but like the Muslim community in America, they too are growing and learning. With time, they will be successful, *insha'Allah*.

Being the informed Muslim that you now are, you should take the knowledge that you have acquired in this book, and expand on it by reading other, more issue-defined books on those topics that most interested you in this book. If you liked the chapter on the presidency, then go to the public library or your local book store and find out what is available for your reading enjoyment. What you should not do is finish this book and put it on a shelf somewhere with the rest of your antique collections and forget about what you learned. No, I have more trust and faith in you for you to do that.

It is my sincere hope that this book will have energized you into taking action and getting involved, whether with a Muslim organization or with one of the political parties in your area. Having connections to both is the best-case scenario because you carry a lot of political clout when you can claim that you have your community behind you, so long as they actually are behind you.

Muslims have much to contribute to this wonderful country. Many of the laws that guide this country have hues, if not direct origins, from *Sharia*. This trend can certainly be continued if Muslims get involved in the political process and not only complain about bad policy, but encourage good policy. The involvement of Muslims in the debate on abortion may perhaps give the pro-life groups the advantage that they need to stop the killing of unborn children. Getting involved in the movement to reform campaign laws may take away much of the power of the pro-Israel lobby, by limiting the amount of influence that can be bought with money. Even the little things make a difference. Muslims can work with their city councils to get streets named after prominent members of their community that have passed away.

In fact, Muslims are making successes every day. In New Jersey, Illinois, California, and Minnesota, Muslims have helped get legislation known as the "*Halal* Food Act" passed, which makes it a crime in those states for any business to claim to sell halal meat when their meat isn't really halal. This is a wonderful project for Muslims in other states to take up because it is an issue that is not controversial, yet at the same time it would be a state law that deals exclusively with the concerns of Muslims.

Let's say a group of Muslims in Pennsylvania want to get a similar law passed. The best thing for them to do would be to get a copy of the actual legislation that was passed by any state with a Halal Food Act on the books. They should then take that bill along with a short proposal to their state representative *and* state senator, show them the legislation, and ask that such a bill be introduced into the state legislature. It is important to go to both the senator and representative because bills have to pass both houses, so if both agree to introduce identical bills then it will make the process much shorter. Politicians like these types of bills because no one can argue against a bill that would protect a religious group from fraud at the grocery store. Also, it makes the politician a hero in the Muslim community if the bill becomes law. So Muslims will most likely throw their political support behind those who had a hand in getting the bill passed, especially those who introduced it.

The levels of success that Muslims reach and the time that it takes to get to those levels depends on their determination to be players in the public square. It also depends on their personal dedication to educate themselves and to work with one another for a common Muslim political agenda for the sake of themselves, their families, and their communities, but first and foremost, for the sake of Allah.

APPENDIX 1: DO YOU KNOW WHO REPRESENTS YOU?

Directions: Try to fill in the blanks without any help. Then do some research and try to fill in the blanks that you missed and correct the ones, if any, that you got wrong. You can choose your state's official website from the list that is provided in this appendix. When you go to this site, search for the section that provides information on who represents you, and once you find it, type in your address and you should receive a complete list of federal, state, and local officials that represent you (*May not be available on all state websites*).

FEDERAL GOVERNMENT

I live in Congressional district_____

My Representative in Congress is_____

The two U.S. Senators from my state are_____ and _____

The Speaker of the House of Representatives is

_____

The Majority Leader of the Senate is

_____

STATE GOVERNMENT

The Governor of my state is

_____

The Lieutenant Governor is
_____

The Secretary of State is
_____

The Attorney General is
_____

The Comptroller/Treasurer is
_____

I live in Senate district _____, and my State Senator is
_____

I live in State House district_____, and my Representative
is _____

LOCAL GOVERNMENT

The Mayor of my city is
_____

I live in Ward/District _____, and my City Councilman is
_____

I live in _____ County, and in County District
_____

My County Board President/Executive is
_____

OFFICIAL WEBSITES FOR ALL 50 STATES & WASHINGTON, DC

Alabama
www.state.al.us

Alaska
www.state.ak.us

Arizona
www.state.az.us

Arkansas
www.arkansas.gov

California
www.ca.gov

Colorado
www.state.co.us

Connecticut
www.ct.gov

Delaware
http://delaware.gov

Florida
www.myflorida.com

Georgia
www.georgia.gov

Hawaii
www.hawaii.gov

Idaho
www.state.id.us

Illinois
www.illinois.gov

Indiana
www.state.in.us

Iowa
www.iowa.gov

Kansas
www.state.ks.us

Kentucky
http://kentucky.gov

Louisiana
www.state.la.us

Maine
www.state.me.us

Maryland
http://maryland.gov

Massachusetts
www.state.ma.us

Michigan
www.michigan.gov

Minnesota
www.state.mn.us

Mississippi
www.state.ms.us

Missouri
www.state.mo.us

Montana
www.state.mt.us

Nebraska
www.state.ne.us

Nevada
www.state.nv.us

New Hampshire
www.state.nh.us

New Jersey
www.state.nj.us

New Mexico
www.state.nm.us

New York
www.state.ny.us

North Carolina
www.ncgov.com

North Dakota
www.state.nd.us

Ohio
www.ohio.gov

Oklahoma
www.state.ok.us

Oregon
www.state.or.us

Pennsylvania
www.state.pa.us

Rhode Island
www.state.ri.us

South Carolina
www.state.sc.us

South Dakota
www.state.sd.us

Tennessee
www.state.tn.us

Texas
www.state.tx.us

Utah
www.state.ut.us

Vermont
www.state.vt.us

Virginia
www.state.va.us

Washington State
http://access.wa.gov

Washington, DC
www.dc.gov

West Virginia
www.state.wv.us

Wisconsin
www.state.wi.us

Wyoming
www.state.wy.us

APPENDIX II: PROFILES OF MUSLIMS IN GOVERNMENT

Dr. Elias A. Zerhouni
Director of the National Institutes of Health, an
agency under the U.S. Department of Health and
Human Services.

Larry Shaw (D)
North Carolina State Senator from District 21.
Chairman of Transportation Committee.

Yaphett S. El-Amin (D)
Member of the Missouri House of Representatives
from District 57.

Rodney R. Hubbard (D)
Member of the Missouri House of Representatives
from District 58.

Honorable David Shaheed
Superior Court Judge in Marion County, IN.
Associated Imam at Masjid Al-Fajr and
Nur-Allah Mosque in Indianapolis.

M.J. Khan (R)
Member of the Houston, TX City Council from
District F. Former president of Islamic Society of
Greater Houston.

APPENDIX III: U.S. PRESIDENTS

PRESIDENT	TERM(S)
1. George Washington	1789-1797
2. John Adams	1797-1801
3. Thomas Jefferson	1801-1809
4. James Madison	1809-1817
5. James Monroe	1817-1825
6. John Quincy Adams	1825-1829
7. Andrew Jackson	1829-1837
8. Martin Van Buren	1837-1841
9. William H. Harrison	1841-1841
	(died first year in office)
10. John Tyler	1841-1845
11. James K. Polk	1845-1849
12. Zachary Taylor	1849-1850
	(died second year in office)
13. Millard Fillmore	1850-1853
14. Franklin Pierce	1853-1857
15. James Buchanan	1857-1861
16. Abraham Lincoln	1861-1865
	(died first year, 2nd term)
17. Andrew Johnson	1865-1869
18. Ulysses S. Grant	1869-1877
19. Rutherford B. Hayes	1877-1881
20. James A. Garfield	1881-1881
	(died first year in office)
21. Chester A. Arthur	1881-1885
22. Grover Cleveland	1885-1889
23. Benjamin Harrison	1889-1893
24. Grover Cleveland	1893-1897
	(separate 2nd term)

PRESIDENT	TERM(S)
25. William McKinley	1897-1901
	(died first year, 2nd term)
26. Theodore Roosevelt	1901-1909
27. William H. Taft	1909-1913
28. Woodrow Wilson	1913-1921
29. Warren G. Harding	1921-1923
	(died third year in office)
30. Calvin Coolidge	1923-1929
31. Herbert Hoover	1929-1933
32. Franklin D. Roosevelt	1933-1945
	(died first year, 4th term)
33. Harry S. Truman	1945-1953
34. Dwight D. Eisenhower	1953-1961
35. John F. Kennedy	1961-1963
	(died third year in office)
36. Lyndon B. Johnson	1963-1969
37. Richard M. Nixon	1969-1974
	(resigned 2nd year, 2nd term)
38. Gerald R. Ford	1974-1977
39. Jimmy Carter	1977-1981
40. Ronald Reagan	1981-1989
41. George H. W. Bush	1989-1993
42. William Clinton	1993-2001
43. George W. Bush	2001-present

Although presidents are elected in November every four years, they do not take office until the following January. President Bill Clinton was elected in November 1992, but he was not sworn in as president until January 1993. Therefore, he served as president from 1993 until George W. Bush was sworn into office in 2001.

APPENDIX IV: RESOURCES ON POLITICS AND GOVERNMENT

Government

FirstGov: The U.S. Government's Official Web Portal
www.firstgov.gov

U.S. House of Representatives
www.house.gov

U.S. Senate
www.senate.gov

The White House
www.whitehouse.gov

The Federal Judiciary
www.uscourts.gov

THOMAS: Legislative Information on the Net
http://thomas.loc.gov

Federal Election Commission
www.fec.gov

Department of Justice
www.doj.gov

Political Parties

The Republican Party
www.rnc.org

The Democratic Party
www.democrats.org

The Libertarian Party
www.lp.org

The Green Party
www.gp.org

Independent

Congress.org: Plenty of information and activism tools on politics and media.
www.congress.org

The Politix Group: Commentary, discussion, and the bi-weekly Political Job Bulletin.
www.politixgroup.org

Political Resources on the Net: Links to national and international political sites.
www.politicalresources.net

Project Vote Smart
www.vote-smart.org

Media

C-SPAN: Public Affairs broadcasting, and so much more!
www.cspan.org

National Public Radio
www.npr.org

Congressional Quarterly Magazine
www.cq.com

Federal News Service
www.fednews.com

The PBS Kids Democracy Project
www.pbs.org/democracy/kids/

Civil Rights and Civil Liberties

American Civil Liberties Union
www.aclu.org

Bill of Rights Defense Committee
www.bordc.org

MAS Freedom Foundation
www.masnet.org

Council on American-Islamic Relations
www.cair-net.org

Muslim Public Affairs Council
www.mpac.org